WHERE TO FOCUS WHEN YOUR LIFE'S A BLUR

CHERYL BIEHL

WHERE TO FOCUS WHEN YOUR LIFE'S A BLUR

MULTNOMAH

Sisters, Oregon 97759

TO BOBBY,
THE MAN I MOST ADMIRE.

CONTENTS

Section 1

Determining God's Direction for You

1

You Can't Do Everything

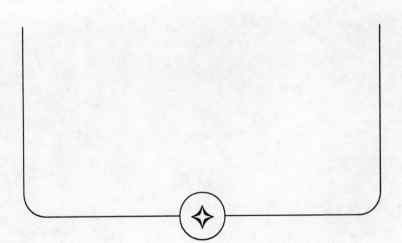

I LOVE YOU," Bobb said as he squeezed my hand. "You're a great travel agent."

American Airlines Flight 29 had carried us at an altitude of seven miles over the icy Atlantic. We were returning home from a trip to Europe with my parents. We were celebrating our wedding anniversaries: their fiftieth and our twenty-fifth.

This trip had been our gift to my parents. Memories which will last a lifetime flooded my mind: a trip down the Rhine; the Matterhorn, gold-tinged at sunrise; a magical Mozart concert in a fortress overlooking Salzburg; a horse-drawn carriage tour through the quaint streets of Vienna; and countless hours of conversation.

During the long plane ride home, I began to list the things I needed to complete in the next two or three months. As the list grew longer, my heart sank lower. When I was finished I had listed forty-three things, one of which was completing this book. Three weeks of personal and office mail was stacked on my desk. There were bills to pay, groceries to buy, thank you notes to write, and messages which I knew would be on the answering machine for me to answer. There would be friends and family who would want my time. Where could I work them in?

I knew that realistically it would be two weeks before I could begin chiseling away at my book deadline. I began to feel depressed and overwhelmed...where should I begin? How could I hope to accomplish all I wanted to do? There was nothing on my list that I could eliminate. The more I thought about it, the more out-of-control I felt. Why had I agreed to the deadline when I knew we'd be gone on this trip for three weeks?

Can you relate with my frustration? Do you ever have more to do than you have time?

Do you ever wonder how you can cope with all that life demands of you?

Do you find yourself juggling the many hats of household taxi, travel agent, correspondent, nurse, tutor, coach, encyclopedia, psychologist, nutritionist, referee, and answering machine?

You're told that every woman needs to fulfill her own needs, so you continue your education, do aerobics, and join a therapy group. As a Christian you're expected to participate in your church activities, so you attend a weekly Bible study, volunteer to make crafts to sell at the annual bazaar, and teach a Sunday school class. And now you feel pulled in a hundred directions by things which all seem to be good and legitimate priorities.

Does this sound familiar? Do you sometimes want to scream, "I CAN'T DO EVERYTHING"?

If so, you are not alone. How can we do all we *need* to do...let alone all we *want* to do?

Life is made up of choices: you make daily choices about what direction your life will take, how you will spend your time, to whom you'll be loyal, what religion you'll embrace, who you will value, how you'll spend your money. But only you can make those choices for your life...and sometimes they seem like weights around your ankles.

If you feel overwhelmed with life's choices, then I have some good news for you. Jesus has issued a personal invitation: "Come to me, all you who are weary and burdened, and I will give you rest. Take my yoke upon you and learn from me, for I am gentle and humble in heart, and you will find rest for your souls. For my yoke is easy and my burden is light" (Matthew 11:28-30).

We can focus our lives in such a way that God carries the heavy side of the burden and we carry the light side. We can let God be the Almighty in our minds and in our lives.

Let me point out that God doesn't promise to take away our problems. He doesn't promise to fix things for us. Quite the contrary. Although Jesus said, "In this world you *will* have trouble," He added, "But take heart. I have overcome the world" (John 16:33). My life's verse, Deuteronomy 31:8, promises: "The LORD Himself goes before you and will be with you; He will never leave you nor forsake you. Do not be afraid; do not be discouraged." God promises to be with us, helping us make wise choices and giving us strength and hope to deal with life's difficulties.

I recently attended a Ligonier Ministries Conference where I heard Dr. Sinclair Ferguson tell an encouraging story from his childhood. When he was about ten years old, he was playing street soccer with some neighbor boys. His team was losing by a wide margin, and there were only five minutes left to play before the boys would be called in for dinner. The situation was desperate. Then the father of one of his teammates came home. The teammate called to his father, "Daddy, come and help us. We're losing." The father took off his suit coat and rolled up his sleeves. Everything changed. Victory was inevitable—the father had been a professional soccer player.

Then in his delightful Scottish accent, Dr. Ferguson drew the obvious parallel: If God be for us, who can be against us. He has promised He will never leave us.

Don't misunderstand: I am *not* saying that because you are a Christian, God is on your side and therefore your business will go better and your life will be trouble-free. But I am claiming that God will be with you in the midst of your pressures. He will give you the strength you need to do what He asks.

This book is an instructional manual to help you get in touch with who you are as a child of God and your desires for your relationship with Him. The steps outlined here will show you how to sort out the responsibilities that are most important for you as a Christian woman. The principle is simple: Go before God to decide what you want to do with the rest of your life, break that down into workable units, and execute those units—one step at a time.

As you pass through different seasons of your life and are introduced to new options, your priorities will change, paving the way for new goals and exciting adventures. This book will *help you* make wise choices for your lifetime, for this particular season of your life, for this year, this quarter, this week, and for today, always keeping focused on God.

Let me assure you it's not my intent to tell you what you *should* do. However, in His Word God has set down some absolutes that we must obey. Those will be discussed as indisputable values and courses of action. A golden thread of spiritual values is woven within the tapestry of this book. If you are not a Christian, my prayer is that you will discover who God is, and how deep, wide, long, and high His love is. He alone can satisfy the heart's deepest longings.

Whatever else this book does, I hope it makes you think. I hope it challenges you to make every minute effective, whether you are working, playing, or resting. Each of us has the same sixty seconds in each minute, the same sixty minutes in an hour, the same twenty-four hours in a day, the same seven days in a week, the same fifty-two weeks in a year, and only God knows how many years we have. Time has a way of slipping by, and

Monday turns into Tuesday, Tuesday to Wednesday, and so on, and at the end of the week perhaps you're not sure what you've accomplished. If you establish your priorities ahead of time, you will most likely do what you determined to do.

But be warned: working through this book will take time. Planning takes time—but lack of planning takes more time. Taking one hour now may save you ten hours or even a hundred hours in the future. Are you willing to make this investment? I hope so.

You may find it helpful to go through this book with a friend or group of friends. Groups can stimulate thought and help eliminate the temptation to put off the suggested exercises. If you work through this manual with other people, your good intentions are more likely to be put into action. The action steps at the end of each chapter are for use with a group or for you to do as you work independently through the system.

Work through this book step by step, completing each exercise before proceeding further. This will help you gradually build a foundation. Different people will require different amounts of time to complete the book and have the system fully operational. If you are tempted to believe that you don't have time to set it up, *remember that the busier you are the more you need such a system to maximize your calendar and clock.*

In the pages that follow you will find principles I use to get more of what I *need* to get done in fewer hours, so I can still have time to do what I *want* to do in those that remain.

They are the principles I used to accomplish the forty-three items I listed after our trip to Europe. That day, while expressing my frustration to Bobb, I told him I wished that someone else had already written this book so I'd know where to begin. His response was encouraging: "Cheryl, I've watched you a thousand times under similar circumstances. Just take notes on how you do it, and you'll have your book." I took his advice and everything got done.

At the end of each day, week, and year of your life, I want you to look back and say, "I like the choices I made for the time I was given. I did what I actually wanted to do, and what I believe pleased God."

1. Make a "to do" list of what you need to do in the next ninety days. Do you feel overwhelmed? Is this a long-term or temporary situation?

2. Look back on the last ninety days. Do you like the choices you made? Are you satisfied with your choices, or do you feel that you "wasted time"?

3. Do you find yourself setting all your goals because of what other people tell you that you should do? Does this conflict with what you want to do?

4. Are you willing to take the time and effort to determine what is best for you to do with the rest of your life?

Focusing Your Heart on God

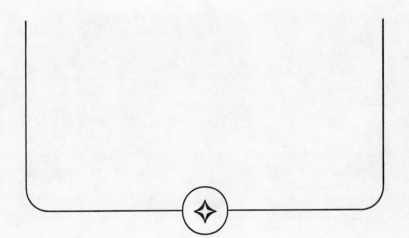

I WANT to move here." Our junior high daughter giggled as she spotted a blonde boy standing in his driveway. We were looking at a house for sale down his street.

Over the next few days Bobb and I talked about whether to make an offer on the house. We checked out the school system—it had a fine reputation. The neighborhood seemed good, and the price was affordable. We made our decision and bought the house.

I busied myself painting and making the house a home. My friend Christine helped me wallpaper our kitchen—I had chosen paper which looked like Dutch tiles. Determined to make my home a showpiece, she insisted that every grouting in that tile pattern be matched perfectly, even on the ceiling.

Thirteen years later, I was making coffee early one morning. As I looked up I noticed an extra horizontal line in the wallpaper located half way between the top of the counter and the bottom of the cupboard. Sure that my sleepy eyes had deceived me, I reached out and touched the wall. My heart sank as I felt a crack in the wall.

Over the next eight weeks, the bottom half of our house slid almost an inch. Large cracks developed everywhere. Our house had been built on a land fill and it was now sinking.

I contacted the builder, an attorney, our homeowners insurance company, a soils engineer, the mortgage lender—everyone who might have an answer to our problem. I accumulated a thick file of paperwork only to learn that in California, after ten years, the homeowner is fully responsible for such problems. The cost of shoring up the hill underneath the house was cost prohibitive.

We were finally able to sell the house to a man whose business is shoring up such problem buildings. This sale protected our credit for which we were enormously grateful, but in the process we lost the equity we had accumulated over the previous fourteen years.

The morning I saw the first crack, my initial reaction was "God, it's your house and whatever you want to do with it is okay." Ten years prior I would have burst into tears. *Why was it so easy for me at that point to hand it to God?* Because I had established the habit of filling my mind with the things of God. Romans 12:2 tells us, "Be transformed by the renewing of your minds. Then you will be able to test and approve what God's will is—his good, pleasing and perfect will." If our minds are filled with thoughts of God then our actions and reactions will reflect that.

What Do You Want?

Years before I had made it my life focus to know God. One morning I had been meditating on Nehemiah. Nehemiah was the cupbearer to the king; he tasted the king's wine first so that if it was poisonous, he would die instead of the king. How would you like that job? (But his fringe benefits were substantial. Read the rest of the book of Nehemiah to see how well the king treated him.)

It was a capital offense to come before the king with a sad face, but Nehemiah had just heard of Jerusalem's wall being in a state of disrepair, and he couldn't fake a smile to save himself. Let's pick up on the conversation between Nehemiah and the king. The king begins:

"Why does your face look so sad when you are not ill? This can be nothing but sadness of heart."

I was very much afraid, but said to the king, "May the king live forever! Why should my face not look sad when the city where my fathers are buried lies in ruins, and its gates have been destroyed by fire?"

The king said to me, "What is it you want?" (Nehemiah 2:2-4).

I meditated that day on the last verse: "The king said to me, 'What is it you want?' "

It was as if my King, my heavenly Father, asked me, "Cheryl, what do you want from Me?" Don't misunderstand me—God had not promised me that He would give me whatever I asked Him for; it was simply an exercise in formulating the deepest desires of my heart. I thought and wrote for perhaps an hour. I remembered other biblical characters who had asked God for favors.

Hannah begged God for a baby boy. "In bitterness of soul Hannah wept much and prayed to the Lord. And she made a vow, saying, 'O LORD Almighty, if you will only look upon your servant's misery and remember me, and not forget your servant but give her a son, then I will give him to the LORD for all the days of his life, and no razor will ever be used on his head' " (1 Samuel 1:10-11).

Solomon asked God for wisdom. "That night God appeared to Solomon and said to him, 'Ask for whatever you want me to give you.' Solomon answered God, 'You have shown great kindness to David my father and have made me king in his place. Now, LORD God, let your promise to my father David be confirmed, for you have made me king over a people who are as numerous as the dust of the earth. Give me wisdom and knowledge, that I may lead this people, for who is able to govern this great people of yours?' " (2 Chronicles 1:7-10).

Esther asked that she would find favor from her husband, the king, as she would plea for her nation. "Then Esther sent this reply to Mordecai: 'Go, gather together all the Jews who are in Susa, and fast for me. Do not eat or drink for three days, night or day. I and my maids will fast as you do. When this is done, I will go to the king, even though it is against the law. And if I perish, I perish' " (Esther 4:15-16).

David asked that one of his descendants would sit on the throne forever: "And now, LORD God, keep forever the promise you have made concerning your servant and his house. Do as you promised, so that your name will be great forever. Then men will say, 'The LORD Almighty is God over Israel!' and the house of your servant David will be established before you" (2 Samuel 7:25-26).

But what did I want? *What was the most important thing I could ask from God?* After much thought and consideration—and God putting a desire within my heart—I realized that *what I wanted most from God was to know Him.* There could be no other answer for me.

That decision provided me with a firm foundation so that when we heard the news that our house was sinking, I was able to rest and not panic. I knew God was faithful and that He was in control.

During the months following my discovery I focused on four characteristics about God which greatly encouraged me.

God Is Sovereign

If there is one thing of which I am certain, it is that God is sovereign. My friend, if He is not sovereign, then He is not God. He has promised in Romans 8:28 that He will, in fact, work *everything* that happens to us for our ultimate good. That good is to mold us into the image of His Son Jesus Christ and to bring glory to God.

The friction comes when He and I differ about what is good for me. How foolish to think that I know more than the Almighty. I can rest, absolutely assured by the knowledge that He is in complete control over every situation in which I find myself and that He has allowed it—in fact ordained it—for my ultimate good.

Being conformed into His image is often uncomfortable or even painful. The way a sculptor works with stone provides a good analogy of this process. Michelangelo contested that in every piece of marble there is a statue yearning to get out. He carved a series of statues which he called the "prisoners." They consist of people, twisted and struggling to free themselves from the marble which holds them captive. Michelangelo believed that the only necessary skill for carving a statue such as "The David" is that of chiseling away the extra marble which is not part of the statue.

I have an excess of marble around me which Christ is chiseling away so that the image of Jesus can be clearly seen. Sometimes it hurts; sometimes I ask why He is allowing this to happen to me; sometimes I pull away, but I know it is always for my good and will make me a truer reflection of Christ.

Confidence in His sovereignty may be the only assurance you will ever have in this life. You may never understand why God allowed something to happen, but you must put your trust in the One who sees the world from the aerial view. Paul tells us that today we see through a glass darkly, but someday, when we stand face to face with Jesus, our vision will be as through crystal-clear glass (1 Corinthians 13:12).

God Is Omnipotent

God is all-powerful—omnipotent. Peter walked on the water to meet Jesus, but when he took his eyes off of Christ, he sunk. If I focus on how impossible a situation is or how insurmountable my problems are, like Peter I will quickly go under. However, if I focus on how big and powerful God is, on how much He cares for me, His child, I am able, like Peter, to walk on the water.

How powerful is God? Is He able to get you through your problem? If you have even an elementary understanding of who God is, you will realize how absurd it is for any Christian to be fearful about anything. In Philippians 4:6 Paul instructs us not to be anxious about anything but to pray about everything. God who knows our needs will supply them. Paul is not saying that we should suppress our anxieties, he's exhorting us to rest assured that God will take care of us. The resolution may not be what we would choose, but God has promised that it will be what is ultimately best for us.

This doesn't mean we sleep in and shirk our responsibilities. When I discovered our house was sinking I pursued every road I thought might lead to solving our problem. When I had done all I could humanly do, I relaxed in the knowledge that it was in God's hands. Our story didn't have a happy, earthly ending: we lost a lot of money. But, I *know* that what happened was for our good. God is in absolute control.

In later chapters I tell more about our upcoming move to Orlando. If God had not pulled up the tap root of my home, I never would have considered moving to Orlando. God worked in my life through a very difficult circumstance to free me to pursue a better situation He had prepared for me.

It is clear how God used this particular crisis for my good. However, that's not always the case. I've never understood why God allowed many of my painful experiences that still don't make sense to me. Yet God is still sovereign. My lack of understanding doesn't change that even a hair's breadth. We absolutely must trust that God is working everything in our lives for our ultimate good. We must always rest in that knowledge and release our problems to Him.

One more thought. I'm concerned about the current popularity among Christians of delving into our past hurts and the injustices done to us. I have seen many people fall into depression as they focused on the negatives in their lives. Don't let this happen to you. I urge you to focus on your eternal status with God and your immeasurable privileges as a Christian who has been redeemed by Christ. Remember Job? When he asked God why he had lost both possessions and health, God did not give him an answer. He showed Job a person: Himself. If I learn to focus on God and who He is, my problems shrivel in comparison. I think you'll find the same is true for you.

God Is Trustworthy

We are quick to say we trust our loving Father—but slow to put it into practice. You and I must learn to abandon ourselves to God. *Abandonment to Divine Providence* by Jean-Pierre de

Caussade is a book God has used to remind me of who He is whenever I wonder why something "unfair" has "happened" to me. Caussade writes:

> If we do not concentrate entirely on doing the will of God we shall find neither happiness nor holiness, no matter what pious practices we adopt, however excellent they may be. If you are not satisfied with what God chooses for you, what else can please you? Does the food prepared for you by God himself disgust you? Well, can you say what other food would not seem stale to someone with so perverted a taste?... What else do you want? Why look elsewhere? Are you wiser than God? Why do you seek anything different from what he desires? Do you imagine, considering his wisdom and goodness, that he can be wrong?... Do you for one moment imagine you will find peace by resisting the Almighty? [1]

When I read those words my view of God snaps into focus. I see how absurd it is to want anything other than what God wants. I'm reminded that I can trust Him to choose what is best. I can say yes, I will accept my circumstances as from His gracious hand, and yes, I will rejoice in them. I can abandon myself to Him.

God Is Omnipresent

God is fully present everywhere—He is omnipresent. Jesus promised He would never leave us. Sinclair Ferguson, in his powerful book, *A Heart for God*, expands on this theme. He points out that when you become a Christian the world's problems do not pass you by. As a Christian you have the assurance that God will be with you in those problems. Life is okay because *God is*. He is the great I AM. If He is with us, Dr. Ferguson explains, then ultimately nothing can be against us. The battle is already won.

Do you remember Elisha's prayer to open the eyes of his servant? The story is found in 2 Kings 6. Elisha is an old, blind prophet but he had "eyes" to see what his servant couldn't. Elisha apprised the Israelite king of war plans being made by the enemy, the king of Aram. After losing a string of battles, the king of Aram thought there was treason among his troops. But upon a thorough investigation, he discovered that Elisha was the informant.

So Aram's king sent soldiers to destroy the old man. When Elisha's servant looked out and saw an army with horses and chariots surrounding the city, he assumed the odds against Elisha and himself were overwhelming. He informed the prophet that they were in serious trouble.

I love Elisha's reply: "Don't be afraid. Those who are with us are more than those who are with them" (v. 16). I can picture the servant's astonished faced. Then Elisha prayed: "O LORD, open his eyes so he may see." Miraculously, God allowed the servant to see what He already had shown Elisha: "hills full of horses and chariots of fire all around them."

God is sovereign, omnipotent, trustworthy, and

omnipresent. Focus on who He is the next time the ground underneath you begins to sink. He won't disappoint you.

Note

1. Jean-Pierre de Caussade, *Abandonment to Divine Providence* (New York: Doubleday, 1975), 31.

3

Seven Habits for Balancing Your Life

MY FAMILY used to spend summer vacation at our cottage on Aylen Lake in Ontario, Canada, about two hundred miles northeast of Toronto. The air was crystal clear—we could see more of the Milky Way against the night sky than nearly anywhere else I have ever been. I remember watching the phenomenal Northern Lights with my boyfriend one quiet evening from a boat which we anchored in the middle of the lake. The stars were unusually bright, allowing us to see more galaxies than I had even known existed, but there was one brighter than all the others—the North Star.

As seasons evolve, the constellations change their positions but the North Star always points us to the north. We've all heard stories of people who get lost in the wilderness but were able to get to civilization because the North Star showed them which way to go. What is true in the physical realm is true in the spiritual realm. As Christians we are to align the direction of our lives with our heavenly Father, our North Star. We are to keep our focus on Him. He will give us direction and balance.

My ability to keep my focus on God and not on my circumstances has been greatly helped by some habits I've established. Because of these habits, when we lost our house I was able to see that it was a short-term problem but that the goodness of God would last forever. You may have time to pursue all of these habits each day; or you may only be able to follow one each day. (Remember, I'm not telling you what you *should* do nor how much time you *should* spend each day; I'm telling you what has helped me keep my life focused on God.)

Habit #1: Spending Time with God Daily

My friend Lynda and I had set our alarms for 6:00 A.M. We had agreed that when we heard our alarms in the morning we would pray for the other person to get out of bed and begin her day with a time of prayer. Later that day we would give account over the phone if we had overcome or yielded to the temptation to sleep in. It seemed to be the crutch we needed, and we both were surprised when soon the extra fifteen minutes we had budgeted was not enough to complete our prayer time.

That was the beginning of my setting aside daily time to be with God, my North Star. It still isn't easy. My bed still entreats me to linger, but years of experiencing the joy of spending time at the feet of our Lord convince me each morning that I want to get up more than I want to sleep.

God doesn't assign points in His cosmic grade book for hours spent in prayer or for tears shed while praying for a friend's health or for hurt feelings experienced as a result of ridicule while sharing one's faith. I am not suggesting that you come to God each morning to have Him put a check mark by your name for some righteous ritual you've completed. I am suggesting that you come to Him each morning to draw close to Him. To focus on Him. To receive *your* focus for the day.

St. Augustine defined prayer as "the affectionate reaching out of the mind for God." Your life—all of it—is to be a prayer to God. Don't, however, use that as an excuse to neglect being still and focusing on the knowledge that He is God. Perhaps you're a night person. I prefer morning so that I can reflect all day on my time with God. You may prefer evening so you can sleep on it and think about it the next day as well. Find the time of least distractions for you. *But recognize it does take time.* It is a commitment.

Habit #2: Picture Yourself Coming before the Holy God of Heaven

God commands us to "be still and know that I am God." Take time right now to picture yourself approaching the throne of Almighty God. What do you picture? Think about His Deity and your humanity; His Holiness and your sinfulness. Worship and praise Him, for He is God Almighty. When you come to Him in prayer, always do so with an attitude of worship and praise.

Before you make requests of God, you must confess any known sins. If there is unconfessed sin

39

in your life, your prayers will go unheard. Isaiah 59:1-2 gives us a solemn warning: "Surely the arm of the Lord is not too short to save, nor his ear too dull to hear. But your iniquities have separated you from your God; your sins have hidden his face from you, so that he will not hear." <u>No sin is worth separation from God.</u>

When there is unconfessed sin in my life it's almost impossible for me to draw near to God. Either I avoid His nearness (if I'm unwilling to confess that sin) or I confess it. But I cannot hold a cherished, unconfessed sin and stand before Him. Confession is an essential step in focusing my heart on God.

If there is unconfessed sin in your life, I urge you to confess it. Open that line of communication with your heavenly Father.

Mark Altrogge wrote a beautiful praise song which describes what happens when we stand in the presence of a Holy God.

> In the presence of a holy God
> I bow down and I adore
> You reveal the secrets of my heart
> And I'm shaken to the core

> In the presence of a holy God
> There's new meaning now to grace
> You took all my sins upon Yourself
> And I can only stand amazed, and I cry[1]

> Holy, holy, holy God
> How awesome is Your name
> Holy, holy, holy God
> How majestic is Your reign

And I am changed
In the presence of a holy God.

In the presence of your infinite might
I'm so small and frail and weak
When I glimpse Your power and wisdom,
    Lord
I have no words left to speak, but I cry

Holy, holy, holy God
How awesome is Your name
Holy, holy, holy God
How majestic is Your reign
And I am changed
In the presence of a holy God.

In the presence of Your glory
All my crowns lie in the dust
You are righteous in Your judgments, Lord
You are faithful, true, and just, and I cry

Holy, holy, holy God
How awesome is Your name
Holy, holy, holy God
How majestic is Your reign
And I am changed
In the presence of a holy God.[2]

Continue to imagine yourself bowing before
Almighty God. (You may want to take notes to
refresh your memory.) You're standing before the
eternal throne, all known sin confessed. As you
stand before Him, be acutely aware of who you
are: a human being, absolutely unworthy to stand
before God the Father on your own merit. God
chose you to be His child for all eternity. He made
it possible through His Son Jesus Christ. Not only

has He forgiven your sins, but He has transferred Jesus' righteousness to you.

You are His child. He cares about you even more than you know how to care and love your own children. He cares about your problems, your hurts, your joys, your victories, your defeats. He invites you to spend time in His presence because He loves you.

When I focus on this, my response is, "Why me, Lord? Why did you choose me to be Your child?" I am eternally grateful. Love overwhelms my heart as I fall to my knees before Him. I am ready to worship Him. I am ready to listen to Him. I am ready to give Him complete control of my life.

All that I am—my assets, strengths, liabilities, fears, anxieties, hurts, past sins, and reputation—all of these I leave with Him.

All that I have—everything I have comes from God. He can take it away at any moment. Today, how does He want to use what He has given me for His glory?

All that I hope to be—my dreams, fantasies, goals. He is free to eliminate or to change any of them. Or He may choose to expand them to bigger heights than I have ever dreamed.

Habit #3: Read God's Word

The next habit which helps me focus my heart is reading God's Word. I like to begin by reading a portion from the Old Testament. It provides me with a historical perspective and gives me insights into things that please God but are not necessarily commanded in the New Testament.

As I read the Old Testament, I am amazed at how slow to learn God's people seem to have been. Over and over again they repeated the same cycle without seeming to learn any lessons. They sinned (usually by placing idols in high places), God placed judgment on them, they repented, and God forgave. Before long they sinned again, and so the cycle repeated itself.

Then I look at my own life. With great distress I realize that I am equally guilty. The only difference is that my idols are not made of wood or stone. But they are idols, just the same, because they take my focus off my God. I worship my own self-centered desires more than I worship my God.

Let me explain. I may be tempted to spend God's tithe on a piece of jewelry or clothing for myself. I may be tempted to ignore a cry for help when I'm tired or to fail to encourage someone with who has a rebellious teenager or a troubled marriage. I may be tempted to exaggerate a story to make myself look superior in some significant person's eyes. I may be tempted to indulge a sinful fantasy. When I give in to these temptations, I have chosen them over God. They have become idols and must be torn down.

Do you remember the account of God asking Abraham to sacrifice Isaac? The report is found in Genesis 22. God promised Abraham that his seed would be as great in number as the sand of the sea. Abraham waited many years and decided to take the matter into his own hands. Ishmael,

Abraham's son, was born to his maidservant Hagar. But God intended for Sarah, Abraham's wife, to bear a son. When Isaac was born, Abraham was one hundred years old. Abraham loved Isaac—and God knew that Abraham's love for Isaac was great so He put Abraham to the test.

When God told Abraham to climb Mount Moriah and sacrifice Isaac, Abraham obeyed God and put Isaac on the altar. When he drew his knife to slay Isaac, an angel appeared. "Abraham! Abraham! Do not lay a hand on the boy. Do not do anything to him. Now I know that you fear God, because you have not withheld from me your son, your only son" (v. 12).

Often I have climbed a Mount Moriah, and like Abraham I must make a sacrifice of what I love. The only difference is, when I draw my knife to kill my idol, no angel comes to stop me as he did with Abraham. Every idol that comes between my God and me *must* be slaughtered.

C. S. Lewis's mentor, George Macdonald, said, "No, there is no escape. There is no heaven with a little of hell in it—no plan to retain this or that of the devil in our hearts or our pockets. Out Satan must go, every hair and feather.

Lewis wrote on this same theme of renunciation in *The Great Divorce*. He tells of an encounter with an angel and a ghost with a red lizard on his shoulder. The angel begs the ghost to let him kill the lizard, who represents sin and evil:

"May I kill it?"

"Honestly, I don't think there's the slightest necessity for that. I'm sure I shall be able to keep it in order now. I think the gradual process would be far better than killing it."

"The gradual process is of no use at all."[3]

This dialog goes back and forth with the angel pleading and the ghost making excuses: He promised to control the lizard and forbid him to speak.

But in the end there was no other way—the lizard had to be killed, as painful as it was to the ghost. After he allowed the lizard to be killed, it was transformed into a silvery white stallion upon which the ghost could ride.

During my quiet times alone with Him, God shows me the red lizards on my shoulder. I must kill them—there is no other way out. Sometimes as they die they are transformed into a strength, but other times they remain dead at my feet. All things apart from God must be sacrificed to Him.

When I finish my Old Testament reading, I move to the New Testament to discover more of what Jesus' character looks like. The more time I spend with Him, looking at His profile, the more I will become like Him. God created me to be a reflection of His son Jesus Christ. When I do this my heart is focused on becoming more like Jesus.

Habit #4: Listen to God through Meditating in the Scriptures

The fourth habit in focusing my heart is listening to God. I ask myself, *What does He have to say to me today?*

The most meaningful method of listening to God that I've come across is meditating on the

Scriptures. This means taking a portion of Scripture and pondering it, praying over it, thinking about it, and perhaps writing about it, and then applying it to my life—*today*.

First I pray and ask God to direct my thinking. I ask Him to show me what lesson He has for me in these particular verses today. Then I go to the Scripture (I begin at the beginning of a book of the Bible and work through it systematically), write down a portion of it, and then write the thoughts that come to my mind about those verses.

I want to make something very clear: These are thoughts from my *mind* that God has illumined. My writing is not anything occultish such as automatic writing or an aimless movement of my hand as with some board games. Neither is my writing a method of the New Age movement. I have simply asked my heavenly Father to fill my mind with His thoughts. If I ask my father for a fish, will He give me a stone? Certainly not our heavenly Father.

Many times God has directed me—through His Word—to some area in my life that needs to be changed. Other times He encouraged me in some discouraging period in my life, or changed the direction I was heading. These experiences came as a result of my being open to what God had to say to me through His Word that day.

I remember well the first time I meditated in this way. I had prayed and asked God to show me in what book He would have me begin. The first epistle of Peter came to mind, and so I began there:

Peter, an apostle of Jesus Christ, to God's elect, strangers in the world, scattered throughout Pontus, Galatia, Cappadocia, Asia and Bithynia, who have been chosen according to the foreknowledge of God the Father…(1 Peter 1:1-2).

First of all, I thought about Peter. He was impetuous and usually spoke before he thought, so he often had his foot in his mouth. Peter had an opinion about everything. But of all the disciples, he was the most adamant about his loyalty and love for Jesus. I identified with all those traits.

Then I imagined my Lord asking me as He had Peter, "Do you love Me?"

"Yes, Lord, You know that I love You."

"Then feed My lambs." Again, in my mind, He asked me if I truly loved Him.

My reply, like Peter's was, "Yes, Lord, You know that I love You."

And again the response, "Take care of My sheep."

A third time He asked me, "Cheryl Biehl, do you love me?"

Like Peter, I became defensive, "Lord, You know all things; You know that I love You." He replied, "Feed My sheep."

At that moment I realized what God wanted me to do in this life: to teach and feed His children—to disciple women. To this day I never tire of doing that.

Some time ago I was leading a small discussion group of women at our church. I was explaining the fall of Adam and that now, because of his fall, we are also born into that same fallen state. But Jesus became the new Adam, and as we are born again, not only are our sins forgiven, but even His righteousness is credited to our account as Christians. One beautiful lady looked at me and said, "The lights just came on. I have never understood that before. For the first time it makes sense to me." One of the greatest thrills of my life is to feed God's lambs and see them digest the food. It truly was an evidence of God's grace that He has allowed me be a part of that process in women's lives.

Today, I study the Scriptures to know God. I read to find what insight others have gained in their pursuit of knowing Him. I love to be in the presence of people who teach me more about Him. I long for the day when I will know Him perfectly, even as I am known—when I see Him face to face.

First John 3:2 teaches, "But we know that when he appears, we shall be like him, for we shall see him as he is." In this life, we know each other through our senses. You are reading this book and are learning to know me because of your sense of sight. If you were listening to me via tape, telephone or in person, I could tell you about myself through your sense of hearing. But you can never know what I am thinking unless I tell you. I know myself directly, but you can only know me secondarily or indirectly. God, however, is not dependent on my communications in order to know me. He alone knows my thoughts even better than I do.

When we see God face to face we will know Him directly and not through our senses. We will know Him as He knows us.

Knowing God takes effort and discipline. What's the result? Peace. Peace that passes all human understanding. Peace because you understand that you are protected and you are secure in Him. Jesus is quoted as saying in John 14:27, "Peace I leave with you; my peace I give you. I do not give to you as the world gives. Do not let your hearts be troubled and do not be afraid."[4]

Habit #5: Use a Prayer Notebook

After I've focused my heart on God, and read and meditated in His Word, I open my prayer notebook.

Perhaps, like me, you can recall promising a friend you'd pray for them about something and then in your busy schedule you forgot to pray. Later that friend thanked you for praying, as God had answered in un unusual way. You felt embarrassed and ashamed because you hadn't remembered to pray at all. Creating and *using* a system of writing down the prayer requests lessens the likelihood of that happening.

Please note that the requests and petitions come long *after* the worship and praise of our Father. We are tempted as desperate human beings to communicate with God only when we desire something from Him. He invites us to come to Him with our needs ("Ask and you will receive, and your joy will be complete," John 16:24), but that should never be the focus of our relationship.

This prayer notebook should never be considered a "gimme" list. Some argue that using a prayer notebook is a little like handing God a grocery list. I agree that it easily can be meaningless. I do use a prayer notebook for the same reason I have a grocery list—I don't want to forget something. But I don't go to the grocery store, hand the manager my list, go back in my car to read a book, waiting for him to collect the items on my list and put them in my trunk. I hold the list in my hand, walk through the aisles, and pull the items off the shelves myself.

In the same way I don't just hand my prayer list to God. I pray through it, asking God to make each person I present to Him become more like Jesus in and through the circumstances in which they find themselves. I ask Him to change some of the difficult situations that these people are faced with, if it be within His will. Jesus taught us to pray saying, "[May] your will be done on earth as it is in heaven" (Matthew 6:10).

Don't ever believe that because you have written down a request, it means you have prayed for it. Some people think that God looks at their notebook daily, so that is all the time they need to spend on that prayer request. The obligation is complete. No! To write it down is simply to *remind you* to pray for it.

Your prayer notebook could be organized in many ways. Some use a clean page for each day's requests; others have separate pages for praise, another for confession, another for intercession (praying for the needs of others), and the last for petition (praying for your own needs).

The method that has been most helpful to me is a yearly notebook. In early January I start a new notebook with fresh pages, simply transferring the unanswered requests to the next year. I use a loose-leaf notebook because it allows me to insert additional pages as needed. I designate one page per person for whom I am praying. I put their name at the top of the page. Then I list general requests that I have for them that I do not expect to be answered conclusively in their lifetime. At the end of the year family members may have four to five pages of requests and answers.

For instance, I pray that my husband would have God's wisdom in his life. Even though I see consistent evidences of that wisdom, I will never be able to point to a day when I say, "It is settled forever, my husband has perfect and complete godly wisdom." I pray for myself to be a godly woman. I've already told you of my prayer to know God. But those prayers will never be completely answered until I stand before Jesus face to face. These are general requests. I have perhaps four to five for each person.

Then I begin listing specific requests, the answers to which can be dated and measured. Health requests, appointments to be successful, houses to sell, trips to be safe, etc., can all be answered yes or no.

I divide the page in half vertically with an imaginary line. On the left side I put the date and the specific request. When I get an answer, I record the date and the specific answer on the same line as the request, but on the right half of the page.

You may ask, "How do you decide who goes into your prayer notebook?" My family is at the top of my list. Also included are:

- ❖ my pastor and his family;
- ❖ other church staff and families;
- ❖ current requests that I know of within the church;
- ❖ close friends and acquaintances;
- ❖ friends of my children;
- ❖ struggling children of my friends;
- ❖ our country and her leaders—the president and members of Congress;
- ❖ whomever God lays upon my heart.

As much as I want to, practically speaking, I don't pray *all* the way through my notebook every day. There are certain people for whom I believe I have a greater responsibility to pray than others. If you're like me and have a large number of people for whom to pray but limited time, you might find it helpful to divide your prayer notebook into sections by days. You might have a daily list which would include the names of family members and close friends for whom you want to pray every day. Then you might have a different list for each day of the week. Monday might be the day you pray for the political arena of our country. Tuesday you might pray for leaders and teachers in the church. Wednesday might be the day you focus on missionaries.

Some days I am able to spend an hour or more praying, while other days I can spend only a few minutes. Some days I spend more time meditating on the Scriptures, and on other days more time is spent in petitioning for the needs of those for whom I believe God would have me pray.

Because I list the answers to my prayers in my notebook, when I pray through it I am reminded of how God answers prayer. It gives me great cause to be thankful. Satan, the enemy of my soul, used to raise questions in my mind as to the validity of my prayers, and caused me to question if God really did answer them. Satan doesn't do this today—I have pages from the last fifteen years which list concrete proof of answers to prayer. What a testament to the faithfulness of God.

Habit #6: Read from a Daily Devotional

I also read from a daily study each morning. I suggest that you choose one which will challenge your thinking such as Ligonier Ministries' *Table Talk* or *Daily Secrets of Christian Living* by George Mueller (compiled by Al Bryant), or Oswald Chamber's classic daily study, *My Utmost for His Highest*. There are many studies available.

While you read these studies be careful not to blindly accept what people teach; search the Scriptures yourself to find answers. Be like the Bereans in Acts 17:11: "Now the Bereans were of more noble character than the Thessalonians, for they received the message with great eagerness and examined the Scriptures every day to see if what Paul said was true."

Habit #7: Read What Other People Say About God

Consider what possibilities you have for additional study. If you have the time in your schedule, you may want to work through a tape series or some challenging book. I once completed a very long and extensive audio tape series on systematic theology taught by Dr. R.C. Sproul. I am so grateful I considered it a priority and committed the time to complete that outstanding series.

I've also read some of the classics by St. Augustine, Jonathan Edwards, and other spiritual giants. Never underestimate the value of what these saints have to teach you. I have included a very short list of books at the back of this book which I recommend to you. Most of these books include a list of other recommended books which you might want to read and purchase. Ask your pastor to recommend some of his favorites to you, or write to me and I'll be happy to accommodate you. I have learned invaluable lessons from godly writers who point me to Christ.

Each day as well as each season of life may differ in the amount of time you can spend in study. But more than anything else, pursue the knowledge of God. It should be your priority. Remember that God is sovereign. He is in absolute control, and He will work *everything* in your life for His ultimate purpose which is your being conformed to His image (see Romans 8:28-29). Focus on Him— your North Star—pray for direction, and rest in Him, knowing that He will direct you according to His perfect will.

Notes

1. This first stanza was composed by the people of Destiny and did not appear in the original lyrics.

2. Song written by Mark Altrogge. Used by permission of Integrity Music.

3. C. S. Lewis, *The Great Divorce* (London: Collins, 1946), 66-69, 89-96.

4. For further study, I would like to refer you to a book which I wrote several years ago, *Scriptural Meditation.*

1. What difficult situation have you experienced which made you realize God's presence in your life?

2. Did any particular attribute of His give you great comfort?

3. How has God used a difficult situation to conform you into His image? If you could go back, would you ask God to remove it from you, also removing the lessons you learned from it?

4. Which of God's attributes brings you the most comfort as you live in this world today?

Section 2

Charting My Course

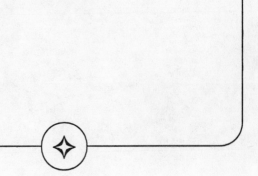

4

What Do I Do with the Rest of My Life?

GRANDMA SHUPE was ninety-six years old when the angels came to carry her to her heavenly mansion. While on earth, she left behind an extraordinary spiritual heritage and memories of a model life.

I remember Thanksgiving dinners at her home in Bad Axe, Michigan. The extended family gathered annually for true thanksgiving to God for a year of prosperity. The twenty-foot-long table was filled with turkey, chicken, pumpkin pie, mincemeat pie, carrot pudding, five vegetables, two kinds of potatoes, cranberry salad, four kinds of pickles, pickled beets, and all the traditional trimmings. The smells from her kitchen still linger in my memory.

I could never hope to fill my grandmother's saintly shoes, but the challenge is mine on Thanksgiving Day to attempt to duplicate her feast. I feel especially close to her in the days preceding the celebration dinner as my kitchen is bustling with preparational activities just as hers once was. Magically, at 2:30 P.M. Thanksgiving Day, everything was carved, cooked to perfection, and served at the ideal temperature.

Several years ago when I reached to grab the proverbial baton of this tradition as it left Grandma's hand, I sat down and did some serious planning. I realized that if I waited until noon on Thursday to begin the dinner, it wouldn't be served by 2:30. If I didn't have a detailed plan of action, the green beans and the rice pudding wouldn't be ready to come off the stove and out of the oven simultaneously.

Just as such a dinner must be planned in advance with precision and painstaking strategy so it is with life. That's why I'm encouraging you now to begin the hard work of planning your life. Once God is clearly in focus, you can begin to form a vision for your life. We'll work backward. First we'll start with the big picture...

What Do You Want to Accomplish before You Die?

What captivates your attention and energy? Don't think yet about what season of life you're in. What would you like to do if there were no restrictions or obstacles? Keep in mind your gifts and abilities as well as preferences. Here are some questions to get you started:

What would you like to be?
Where would you like to go?
How will you get there?
What would you like to do?

Whom would you like to help before you die?
What gifts and abilities has God given to you?
What are your desires?
Where would you enjoy living?

Think carefully before you answer. If there were no other people in the world watching you; if you were not trying to impress or please anyone else, what would you do or say? Would your choices be any different? Remember, the choices you make must please God alone. He must be your "audience of One."[1]

This doesn't mean you have permission to hurt or offend other people, or even be inconsiderate of them. But if, in choosing your path in life, your eyes really are on the North Star and other people misunderstand or try to coerce you into doing something else with your life, then it's their problem—not yours. Someone else may be trying to manipulate you or live their life vicariously through you. Don't let another person paralyze or sidetrack you from what you believe God would have you do.

If someone tries, listen and consider it carefully; bring it before God in prayer and re-evaluate. You alone must answer to God for the choices you make. The question to ask yourself in determining your life's ambitions is: "Who am I trying to please? Who is my audience?" Make your choices carefully and cautiously.

You might be thinking that this is for everyone but you because you have very few talents. You may look at someone else and say, "If I had her abilities—or beauty or money—I could do anything. But not me; I am no one special." I believe this kind of thinking insults God. He made you in His image. He can help you accomplish things you never dreamed possible.

Recently I heard a young woman give her testimony and sing.

Her body was severely impaired: her mother had attempted to abort her. Yet this young woman wasn't bitter and sang to the glory of God. Her physical drawbacks are obvious to all, yet she is doing what she can—and it is significant.

We've all heard the story of Joni Erickson Tada. I admire her courage, but even more I admire her determination to obey God. Because of her accident and her response to it thousands of people have come to God.

What both these women have accomplished has very little to do with their talents and abilities—it has everything to do with the power and grace of God. When we obey God, we can do much more than we ever thought possible. What is your passion? If it is God-given He will help you accomplish it.

Getting It Down on Paper

It may take some time to answer these questions. Take the time—the answers are foundational for what you decide. I'd encourage you to write them down and maybe even talk them over with your spouse or a close friend. Most importantly, pray about them.

It would be so simple if we had the option of calling God on the phone and asking Him to tell us what He wants us to do. Unfortunately we don't have that option. The truth is, God isn't going to write out your goals for you as He did for Moses.

But He has given us prayer as a means of communication, the Bible to follow as His written guide, the Holy Spirit to teach us and remind us of truths, and a brain which He expects us to use. James 1:5 promises: "If any of you lacks wisdom, He should ask God, who gives generously to all without finding fault, and it will be given to him."

On pages 66 and 67 is a chart titled "LIFE FOCUS." It has been filled in so that you have a model to study and follow. Before you read any further, take a moment to look over the chart.

On pages 162 and 163 is a blank LIFE FOCUS chart for you to fill in—feel free to copy this chart and any others. This chart has seven categories for you to fill in. When you are ready to complete it be as accurate and thorough as you possibly can. I suggest using pencil as it will make changes easier and give you freedom to write down ideas which you don't set as priorities but will later. You'll be thinking through seven areas of life:

   ✧ Spiritual
   ✧ Family/Marriage
   ✧ Professional/Mental
   ✧ Physical
   ✧ Financial
   ✧ Personal Development
   ✧ Social/Friends

LIFE FOCUS

Before I die, I want to...

	BE:	DO:
SPIRITUAL	Focused on God	Summer missionary project Bible study at work
FAMILY/ MARRIAGE	Wife — happily married, Mother of 3 children	Raise the family Support children thru college Family vacations Trip with my parents
PROFESSIONAL/ MENTAL	A nurse	Floor nurse in hospital
PHYSICAL	120 pounds	Aerobics 5 days per week Bicycle trip to San Diego
FINANCIAL	Comfortable Responsible to pay bills Generous	Set up budget and live by it
PERSONAL DEVELOPMENT	An encourager	Learn to ride a horse Learn to speak Spanish Take piano lessons
SOCIAL/ FRIENDS	A good listener to my friends	Lunch once a week with a friend Have a Christmas party

Before I die, I want to…

HAVE:	HELP:	
Daily time of worship & prayer	*Pray with hurting patients* *House unwed girls in crisis* *pregnancies*	**SPIRITUAL**
"Happy" husband & 3 children	*Emotional & physical support* *for family*	**FAMILY/** **MARRIAGE**
Nursing degree	*People who are physically* *hurting*	**PROFESSIONAL/** **MENTAL**
Cholesterol level under 200	*My family by serving nutritional* *meals*	**PHYSICAL**
Home paid for	*Homeless people* *Church giving* *Trust for each grandchild*	**FINANCIAL**
		PERSONAL **DEVELOPMENT**
	A friend's child on a summer *missionary trip*	**SOCIAL/** **FRIENDS**

Spiritual. This area infiltrates every part of your life and will affect every other category. For instance, because you are a Christian, you must maintain honest professional relationships. You can never embrace a dog-eat-dog mentality to climb the corporate ladder. There is nothing intrinsically wrong with reaching the top rung of that ladder, but to push someone else down to accomplish it is not obeying the biblical mandate to love your neighbor as yourself.

Even though the spiritual pervades all the areas, it also deserves to be considered separately. One priority you may wish to include in the "do" column may be to read your Bible systematically through from front to back cover. Another may be to make a study of what the Bible teaches about grace or fear. Tapes and seminars are other options you might consider.

Family/Marriage. I've put family and marriage into one category, but I actually believe you need to plan for both family and your marriage.

Focus on the Family has a wide selection of materials available to help you make your family times meaningful. *The Family Discipleship Handbook: 365 Easy Activities to Nurture your Child's Spiritual Growth* by Dr. Jerry MacGregor is also a valuable resource.

I would like to add a note of caution here. It's easy to become so focused on your family that you neglect your relationship with your husband. To keep your marriage strong you and your husband need to be alone. Plan interesting times together so that your marriage never becomes dull. Enjoyment or entertainment doesn't need to be costly. As you make goals for this area, remember that time with your children is irreplaceable—and will soon be history.

Professional/Mental. This is an area which may need to take a back seat if you have preschool children. (I talk more about our seasons of life in the next chapter.) When your children are in school you might want to take some community college courses in your professional area or prepare to begin a new profession when you have more time to devote to a career outside your home. Some women find they enjoy working part-time while their children are home.

Physical. You will need to custom fit this section to your season of life. If you have preschool children you already get a lot of exercise chasing those little ones around the house. Later, when you drive them in the car or wave good-bye to them as they take your car, you may need to join a gym, aerobics class, or use a video exercise tape. Perhaps you want to lose or gain weight or become more heath conscious in your diet.

Financial. This will vary with your season of life, level of income, and number of children. Do you need to save for your child's college education or for your retirement? Would you like to increase your tithe?

Personal Development. This is another area which varies considerably with the seasons of life. When your children are very young, this one may not be as time consuming as in later years when you have more time to develop your own interests.

For instance, when your children are grown you may wish to become an expert in a particular subject, language, or skill. There are a wide variety of learning tapes available which can result in a great deal of personal development. Local college campuses offer many interesting areas to pursue. The library is always a great source of knowledge.

Social/Friends. What would you like to do socially before you die? Perhaps you'd enjoy having an annual Christmas party, or traveling to Europe with your favorite friends. In this section you might list several people with whom you would like to become friends. You might include helping to support a friend's missionary trip to Hungary or Russia. Perhaps you would like to make a goal of being "fully present" to whichever friends may need it as they struggle with their children or marriage.

Let's Get Started

Remember that not all the boxes need to be filled out completely. Write down the goals in the areas which are important to you. There are no right or wrong answers or correct lengths of lists. Pray and ask God to show you what would please Him. The LIFE FOCUS chart is simply a vehicle to help you look beyond present circumstances and see a long-term picture of what you'd like to accomplish with your life.

If you're having difficulty coming up with things to put in the boxes, try to remove restricting limits. What would you like to be, do, have, or help if you had absolutely unlimited funds available, you knew you couldn't fail at whatever you chose to do, and you were responsible to God alone. God doesn't limit our creativity as long as it stays within His behavioral boundaries. His purpose for us is to be conformed to His image. Use your mental capacities to determine a creative plan which could allow you to realize those dreams which are most important to you as you seek God's perspective.

If you are married, I encourage you to talk over your priorities with your husband. Ask for his input. Listen to his opinions and concerns. The Bible teaches that "the two shall be one," and as Christian women we must follow that biblical mandate.

You are a part of a family unit which works together. It is not wrong to experience independent areas of fulfillment, but you are responsible before God to complete the obligations of your role in the family. You are to be a part of contributing unity rather than divisiveness or autonomy within the family unit. If you find your goals are undermining the well-being of the family, you must be willing to alter or postpone yours for the good of the whole family. Again, go before God and sincerely seek His will for your life.

Choosing Ladders

As I mentioned in chapter 1, this book is a manual to help you sort out what is important to you and then to help you with a plan to make those things become reality. To get the maximum benefit from this book, work through the Life Focus chart before going on to the next chapter. If you read ahead without actually participating in the assignments, you may be tempted to skip some essential steps. The temptation will be to put the book down and give up. Don't. Take the book one step at a time.

Spend time working and reworking the LIFE FOCUS chart; weigh carefully each item listed. Ask yourself how important this particular thing actually is to you. Remember, however, that it is written in pencil, and a year, month, or week from now, you still have the freedom to change it completely if you are exposed to some new and challenging idea or if the priority you chose has lost its appeal.

Search the Scriptures to determine if they speak directly to the particular issue in question. For example, the Bible speaks clearly to the issue of an extra-marital affair. That is out of the question for any Christian. It does not, however, directly tell you if you should live in Missouri or Texas, or what kind of car to drive. Seeking the counsel of an older and wiser Christian, however, may lend a perspective on the situation that you hadn't considered. They may bring in biblical principles such as financial responsibility which will make obvious the decision to purchase a more economical automobile.

God is sovereign, and He certainly has the ability to stop us if He has something for us to do other than what we are planning. For instance, Paul the apostle planned several times to go to Rome and each time he was prevented from doing so. When he finally arrived, he was a prisoner in chains. Paul was listening to God and so must you.

Filling out the LIFE FOCUS chart is like looking at different ladders to climb and different walls to lean those ladders against. If you don't choose ahead of time, you might find yourself climbing the first ladder you see, and not liking where it took you when you reach the top.

I suggest you follow Habakkuk's example. Habakkuk was upset because God wasn't answering in the way or in the timing that he thought was best. But Habakkuk knew if he had a difference with the Almighty, it was a problem with his thinking and not God's. So he did a very wise thing—he climbed his tower and waited to get God's perspective.

You and I can do the same.

Note

1. I first heard of the concept of an "audience of One" from Os Guinness, speaker and writer.

1. Who is your audience? Are you living life to please other people or God?

2. As you completed your LIFE FOCUS chart, did anything emerge as a priority which you were not even aware was a desire?

3. If you are married, what is the relationship you have with your husband in regard to setting your own goals versus fitting into his?

5

Making the Most of My Seasons of Life

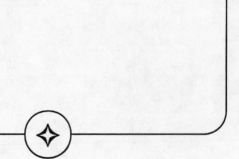

P ICTURE THE FOLLOWING scenario.

"Can I join the Girl Scouts, Mommy? Can I? Can I, pleeeeease?" Susie begged her mother.

Mary remembered her Girl Scouts days and agreed the commitment would be good for Susie. Soon it was time for the annual Girl Scout cookie sale and Saturday afternoon found Mary and Susie at a local grocery store, smiling at everyone who was going in and out. Susie's cookie sales were high and she gained recognition in her troop. Throughout the years, Mary made it a priority to spend time with Susie in Scout pursuits.

Now let's move the scene forward ten years.

Susie is in college and Mary spends her time teaching a Bible study at church, entertaining friends, and traveling with Tom. One day the Girl Scout troop leader calls and asks Mary to help sell cookies this year. She looks at her calendar which is full, and decides it is a "good" but not a "best" way to spend her time now that Mary is no longer a Girl Scout. When Mary's circumstances changed, so did her priorities.

Solomon explained it several thousand years ago in Ecclesiastes 3:1 "There is a time for everything, and a season for every activity under heaven." It's true. Each season of a woman's life has its own unique characteristics—and most of us go through quite a few seasons of life.

A young single adult woman, for example, has no immediate family for whom or to whom she is responsible. If she marries, she exchanges a bit of her freedom for the relationship she desires with one man. When they have children, her priorities change considerably because she now has people who are dependent on her for their very existence. As those children grow up and become more independent, her responsibilities continue to change. Teenagers are almost autonomous (sometimes not as much as they would like to think) and so in this season a woman has time to pursue her own interests. Once the children leave home, she will have time to pursue priorities outside the family.

Below, I have listed most of the seasons a woman may pass through in her lifetime. It's not exhaustive and certainly not true of every woman. I have divided the seasons according to the relationships women have with family members. They may overlap, as one child in your family may be a preschooler, while another is in elementary, junior high, or even high school.

1. Childhood
2. Adolescent
3. Single Adult

4. Married without Children
5. Family with Preschool Children
6. Family with School-age Children
7. Family with Teenage Children
8. Empty Nesters
9. Grandparents
10. Widow

Other possible seasons:

Caring for Elderly Parents
Single Parent
Blended Family
Divorced with No Children

Clearly, not everyone passes through each of these seasons. Single women, of course, don't go through these particular seasons and so their priorities throughout their lives are different from those of married women. Single women are able to define what they would like to do without regard for others for whom they are responsible or to whom they are accountable.

Going through the Seasons of Life

Each season has delights of its own. There is nothing to compare with the feeling you have when you walk into your baby's room after a nap and she looks at you and says, "Ma ma ma ma ma."

I remember the day when our daughter, on her sixteenth birthday cheered for her first football game, and the boy she was "crazy about" took her off the field early to begin a five-dates-in-one-day marathon which I had secretly planned for her. What fun I had as each boy waited in the driveway for her as she was to return from her previous date. I love surprise parties.

But each season also has its challenges. Another memory I have is one of lying on the floor, playing with our son of six months. I tickled him and we both laughed and giggled with sheer delight—until he threw up green peas right into my mouth. (That was not an experience I want to repeat.)

When my children became teenagers I experienced many anxious moments as they tried to discover who they were in this confusing world. The challenge of rearing teens is knowing when to intervene and when to step back and allow your child to learn from experiencing the consequences of a poor choice. Confusion is normal for teens as they cut the "apron strings" and gain independence as they try to understand who this person is who is living inside this rapidly changing body.

I have one word of caution—especially if you have teens: *Never* betray the confidence of your family.

One day I was discussing a problem with our junior high school son. He asked if I had shared this situation as a prayer request with my friends. I said I had because I wanted their prayer support. His words penetrated deep into my soul: "That's nothing but a gossip line. You want me to be a certain way because you want to impress your friends." He was right—and I've never forgotten it.

God doesn't need your friends to be informed about your child's or husband's needs. He knows the details far better than you or your friends do.

Ask them to pray that God's will is done in the lives of your family. Protect family members by allowing their business to remain their private affair. Just because you happen to be their mother doesn't mean you have the right to discuss their personal lives with your friends. Share anything you want to about your own personal life, but no one else's. Don't try to mold them into the image you have in mind for them; let God mold them into His image.

My Husband Wants Me to Work...

I often hear from women that their husband wants them to work outside the home...and the woman prefers not to until her children are gone. If you find yourself in this situation, I encourage you to talk with your husband about why he feels as he does.

Does he believe you would enjoy the stimulation of the work environment? Perhaps he sees career women at his office who seem fulfilled and happy and he thinks, "I know my wife could do that, too. I'll bet she'd like the challenge and social interaction with other people."

Is he concerned because he feels you are becoming lethargic and living up to less than your potential? Is he concerned about your financial situation?

Whatever his reason, if your desire is not to work, explain your reasons to him. Show him your seasonal goals. Point out why you believe your being at home is critical for the best interest of the family at this time—but that the need will change as your children get older. Show him you *do* have a plan and not working at this point is a part of it. This may diminish his apprehensions.

I Have to Work...

I've talked with many women who felt they had to work even though neither they nor their husbands wanted them to. My niece and her husband were in this situation. Before their baby came, Carol had a promising career and thought that she would put the baby in day care. However, when he was born, Carol had a change of heart and wanted to stay home with him. She and her husband felt strongly enough about it that they moved to a more affordable house so she didn't need to work.

If you think you must work but would prefer not to, try to be creative. Sit down with your husband and brainstorm about ways that you can cut expenses or make money from your home. Be creative.

Sometimes there are no options, however. If that's your situation, I suggest that you carefully reconsider your seasonal charts. This is a temporary situation. Can some of what you hope to accomplish with your life be postponed to another season?

Again be flexible and creative with your time, money, and energy.

Fulfilling Your Life Focus in Your Season of Life

At the end of the chapter are two charts titled "SEASONS OF LIFE." The first is a sample for you to review in helping you complete your own, which you will find on pages 84 and 85. Study the sample chart for ideas and clarification. Notice how the sample LIFE FOCUS priorities (pages 66 and 67) are being woven into the SEASONS OF LIFE chart. Remember to use pencil so you can change your goal as new information occurs in your life.

Put the season of life in which you currently find yourself in the box just to the right of the one which reads "Season of Life" and complete the columns to the right of that with what you expect your future seasons to be. With your SEASONS OF LIFE chart in front of you, get out your completed LIFE FOCUS chart. Which ambitions are feasible for you to accomplish in your current season of life? Choose those which are most meaningful to you and place them in the SEASONS OF LIFE chart where appropriate. Repeat that process until all of the priorities listed in the LIFE FOCUS chart are on your SEASONS OF LIFE chart. Use the sample charts to find examples of how this process works.

As you work on your chart, remember your North Star. Seek God's direction. Ask Him to show you what is best for you and what you can do to become more like Him. He tells us that as we are open to His leading, He will give us the desires of our hearts. He puts desires within us and then gives us the joy of seeing them realized. As time goes by, you will probably discover that a few of those things which you listed lose their importance. Others will gain value.

SEASONS OF LIFE

SEASON> OF LIFE	FAMILY WITH PRESCHOOL CHILDREN	FAMILY WITH TEENAGE CHILDREN
SPIRITUAL	Focused on God Attend morning Bible study once per week 30 min. personal time with God each day	Focused on God 45 minutes personal time with God each day
FAMILY/ MARRIAGE	Family vacations	Family vacations
PROFESSIONAL/ MENTAL	Take 2 classes per term toward RN degree	Take 2 classes per term toward RN degree
PHYSICAL	Aerobics 3 days per week	Aerobics 5 days per week Bicycle trip to San Diego
FINANCIAL	Give tithe to church Savings for children's college	Give tithe to church Savings for children's college
PERSONAL DEVELOPMENT	Learn to ride a horse Take piano lessons with children	Learn to speak Spanish with children Take piano lessons with children
SOCIAL/ FRIENDS	Dinner and evening with friends once per month	

SEASONS OF LIFE

Empty Nester	Grandchildren	<Season of Life
Focused on God Summer missionary project House unwed mothers 1 hr. daily personal time w/God	Focused on God Pray with hurting patients 1 hr. daily personal time w/God	SPIRITUAL
Support children through college Trip with my parents	Trip with children and grandchildren	FAMILY/ MARRIAGE
Finish RN degree Work in hospital	Become floor nurse	PROFESSIONAL/ MENTAL
Aerobics 5 days per week	Walk 3 miles per day	PHYSICAL
Finish paying for home before retirement Give tithe, plus extra projects	Finish paying for home before retirement Give tithe, plus extra projects Buy bonds for each grandchild	FINANCIAL
		PERSONAL DEVELOPMENT
Lunch once a week with a friend Have a Christmas party	Lunch once a week with a friend Support a friend's child in a missionary project	SOCIAL/ FRIENDS

This was certainly true in my case. When I had preschool children, I knew that someday I would like to write and speak, but it was not best at that time. Those ambitions would have to wait until my nest was empty. However, I didn't feel cheated that I couldn't realize those goals right then because I believed that my priority at that time was to be a loving and caring mother to my children. I knew my books and speaking could wait until our children were older.

So, just because they can't be accomplished right now, don't limit what you write down as goals. Consider *when* you will be able to pursue them and write them in the section of the chart for that season. That will help you find satisfaction in the goals you pursue today.

Choosing "Best" over "Good"

If you feel overwhelmed by the number of interests you have and are feeling you can't do it all, sort out the best from the good. We will look more carefully at this distinction as we move into the next chapters. For now, let me say that you *can't* do everything, but you *can* do what is best and most important for you. Few of us are tempted to allow bad things to keep us from achieving the best, but good things certainly can and do often consume our time, robbing of us of what we want to do most. Weigh each item you listed on the LIFE FOCUS chart. Is it a "good" or a "best" for you?

In Philippians 1:9-11 Paul tells the saints in Philippi of his prayer:

> And this is my prayer: that your love may abound more and more in knowledge and

depth of insight, so that you may be able to discern what is *best* and may be pure and blameless until the day of Christ, filled with the fruit of righteousness that comes through Jesus Christ—to the glory and praise of God (emphasis mine).

Paul prays that they would be able to discern what is best for them. How were they to determine that? By their love abounding more and more in knowledge and depth of insight. In other words, by seeking God's face they would gain insight and know what was the best for them. How would that benefit them? It would cause them to be pure and blameless until the day of Christ, filled with the fruit of righteousness. If we always choose what is best, we will be pure and blameless.

Again, let me emphasize that this is a personal value judgment and can only be determined *for* you *by* you. An ambition which is a best for you may be a good for someone else, and vice versa. Something which is a good for you in one season of life may be a best for you in another.

Be Flexible!

Throughout your life, be open to new options. Technology is rapidly increasing, bringing unlimited opportunities. Only the Lord knows what tomorrow will bring. Some day you may find your greatest fulfillment working in some position that isn't even available today. As you mature in your relationship with God and knowledge of Him, your desires may change. Let God mold these desires within you; allow Him to bring change.

I have recently desired to attend seminary. I am not sure why or how God will use that training in my life—but I'm sure when the time comes, I'll know how He'll use it. I am having to be flexible and open—sure of the short-term but unsure on the long-term. I view my LIFE FOCUS and SEASONS OF LIFE charts as guides—they are not set in stone. That's why I use pencil. I abandon myself to God every day and if He brings something to my life other than what is on my list, I change things around to accommodate that. Because I plan so carefully, I have time for flexibility and interruptions.

In fact, I'm having to flex right now. It's time to get my yearly, quarterly, and weekly targets on paper, but I need to get ready to move across the country. I have a long list of ends that *need* to be tied before the move. When I add things I *want* to do in the process, the list grows even longer. The only way I can climb this mountain is to break it down into workable units and ascend one small step at a time. But it is possible; I've used this process many times and it works. Try it and you'll see.

Before going on to the next chapter, take the time now to get your seasonal priorities on paper.

1. Think of an example in your own life where something was a "best" in a past season, but is now only a "good." Will it ever be a "best" again?

2. Is there something over which you have felt resentment because you couldn't pursue it in this season? Does it relieve your anxiety to know it is only being postponed and not discarded?

3. What "good" thing is actually robbing you of a "best" in your life? Can you eliminate it?

4. After completing your SEASONS OF LIFE chart, are you fully satisfied with what you are doing in this particular season of your life, realizing that other seasons will afford you different options?

6

A Plan That Works

IT'S APRIL and we're not moving until January—nine months away. No problem, right? No worries, right? Lots of time, right?

Wrong.

How many times have you put off a project and then before you knew it, the deadline arrived. You scrambled to get it done; you drank lots of coffee throughout the night to finish. You panicked. I know the feeling—I've been there, too. I've left lots of ends loose. But I've learned from my mistakes and have succeeded in minimizing the likelihood of having such stress in the future.

By now you probably know what I'm going to say: The key lies in the planning.

In order to determine a plan to assist you in achieving your priorities you'll need to work backward starting with your priorities in life:

✧ What have you determined is important for you to accomplish in your life-time (LIFE FOCUS chart)?

✧ Where have they been plugged in on your SEASONS OF LIFE chart? Which ones fit into your current season of life?

Goals vs. Priorities

You've already established your personal focus before God and determined the *general priorities* for each of the seasonal categories of your life. The next step is to set some *specific goals* which will help you fulfill your priorities. Goals are targets for the future. They stretch you beyond what you are currently achieving.

Here are some points to keep in mind while writing out your goals:

Goals must be realistic. Perhaps in the past you have set unrealistic goals so you failed to achieve them. Now you avoid them. It is more comfortable not to set any goals than not to reach those you have set. If that's what has happened to you, try setting only a few attainable goals and when those are reached, add more. Allow yourself the satisfaction of reaching those you have set.

Goals must be measurable. For instance, if you write that your goal is "to be thin" you will have a hard time assessing whether or not you achieve your goal. It is vague and impossible to measure. However if you write "maintaining XXX pounds" you have written a measurable goal. Every morning as you step on the scales, you are aware if you have wavered a pound from that ideal weight. Set your goals specifically and measurably so you know when you have reached them.

Setting Goals for This Season

Specific goals are usually set within our current season of life. It would be a monumental task to establish actual goals for each season of your future. And it most likely will be an exercise in futility because of all the changes that will take place. (An exception would be if you are approaching the next season of your life. If that describes you, you might need to make goals that will help ease your passage through the seasonal doors.)

As you work to identify your current goals, use your SEASONS OF LIFE chart. Before you begin, approximate the number of years you have remaining within the current season. Look at your chart and try to write specific goals for the priorities you identified for this particular season. Use the same principle you used in the last chapter with the LIFE FOCUS and SEASONS OF LIFE charts: Take one priority from the seasonal chart. Break it down into steps. Write those steps on your seasonal chart under the years you would like to accomplish them. Break those down even smaller and place those steps on your quarterly charts.

If you are having trouble squeezing everything into the years within this current season, ask which things could be deferred to a future season, or what you could begin now and finish later. For instance, you may begin the goal of earning an educational degree by taking one course each semester while you are in the "family with preschool children" season. As you enter the "family with school-age children" season, perhaps you can handle two classes per semester, and actually finish the degree when you move into the "empty nesters" season.

Try to be creative about how you will fulfill those goals which are important to you. Don't give up too easily. Susan was a mother of two preschool children who had what appeared to be two conflicting goals. One was that she stay at home with her children, the other was they would put money away for a college education for their kids. The trouble was once they paid their tithe and living expenses there wasn't enough left for them to put money away. So Susan and her husband talked it over and she decided that she could earn some income by babysitting three or four other children during the week. It wasn't much, but it was a start until her children were in school.

As always, keep your North Star clearly in mind. What has God burdened your heart with? You may find that some things take on a much higher priority than others. Don't be afraid to use an eraser. Your value as a person does not diminish if you decide that one or several of the priorities are not as important as they first appeared and so you aren't willing to commit your valuable time to it. (I know I keep repeating this point—but I want to make sure you get the message.)

Be true to yourself and what you want to accomplish. Remember—it is God who puts the desires into your heart as you go before Him, seeking to please Him. Other people may try to set your priorities and goals for you, but you must determine what is most important to you, what brings you the most satisfaction when achieved, and what God would be most pleased with your accomplishing.

Setting Goals for this Year

When do you fill out your YEARLY FOCUS charts? When you enter into a new season of your life. At that time you can establish your yearly goals for *each year* in that season. I suggest that you review them at least annually to make necessary adjustments.

Take a moment now to study the sample YEARLY FOCUS chart on pages 98 and 99.

As you make yearly goals consider your unique time demands within this particular season. For instance, if you have children in junior high or high school, a substantial amount of your time is demanded as you taxi them to places they need to go. When they secure their own driver's license, and you feel comfortable letting them drive alone, you will have more time to make other goals a priority.

As you fill in this chart, keep in mind the following:

Consider the necessities first. If you have preschool children, you need to nourish and care for them. Changing diapers, bathing babies, and wiping running noses is time consuming. Don't set unrealistic goals in those years which, if not completed, will cause you frustration and discouragement.

YEARLY FOCUS

YEAR>	*1990*	*1991*
SPIRITUAL	*Keep focused on God* *15 minutes daily personal time with God*	*Keep focused on God* *15 minutes daily personal time with God*
FAMILY/ MARRIAGE	*Give birth to child #2* *Be the best mother I can be* *Weekend away with husband once each quarter*	*Be the best mother I can be* *Weekend away with husband once each quarter*
PROFESSIONAL/ MENTAL		
PHYSICAL		*Get weight back to normal after pregnancy*
FINANCIAL	*Tithe to church*	*Tithe to church*
PERSONAL DEVELOPMENT		
SOCIAL/ FRIENDS	*Dinner and evening out with friends once a month*	*Dinner and evening out with friends once a month*

SEASON: FAMILY WITH PRESCHOOL CHILDREN

1992	*1993*	<YEAR
Keep focused on God *15 minutes daily personal time* *with God*	*Keep focused on God* *15 minutes daily personal time* *with God*	SPIRITUAL
Be the best mother I can be *Weekend away with husband* *once each quarter*	*Give birth to child #3* *Be the best mother I can be* *Weekend away with husband* *once each quarter*	FAMILY/ MARRIAGE
		PROFESSIONAL/ MENTAL
		PHYSICAL
Tithe to church	*Tithe to church*	FINANCIAL
		PERSONAL DEVELOPMENT
Dinner and evening out with *friends once a month*	*Dinner and evening out with* *friends once a month*	SOCIAL/ FRIENDS

Don't forget yourself. Often we get so involved in meeting the needs of other people that we forget to take time to refresh ourselves. If you have flown on a commercial airline lately, you will recognize the speech which the flight attendants recite just before takeoff. It goes something like this, "In the event of a loss of cabin pressure, an oxygen mask will automatically be lowered. If you are sitting beside a child, first secure your own mask and then his or hers." Why would they advise you to do that? Are they promoting an "adults over children" philosophy? Hardly. They realize that unless you as the adult are getting the oxygen you need, you will be of no help at all to the child, and you both could die.

Jesus, filled with absolute love and compassion, went to the mountains to spend time with His Father in prayer to renew His weary body and soul. When the crowd pressed in upon Him, he suggested to the disciples that they all get away from the crowd and go to the mountains alone. If Jesus took time to replenish His soul, shouldn't we?

Are you getting enough "oxygen" in your life to be of maximum benefit to those around you? It is not a selfish gesture to set goals which allow you to "refill your cup." Just as an empty tea kettle will crack or melt as the heat under it is turned up, so you will break as the heat of life is turned on high if your cup is dry.

How do you refresh your soul? Set realistic goals which make room for you to nurture yourself. If you have small children, perhaps you can trade babysitting time with a friend or neighbor to allow each of you a morning or a day every week to meet with a friend for lunch, read a good book, shop for yourself without children, get a complete make-over, take a luxuriating bubble bath—uninterrupted—or to take a walk in the park.

Don't forget others. Make time in your life to give to people. One gift to others that has immeasurable significance is encouragement. Bobb's high school English teacher recognized his ability to conceptualize and write. She commented to him one day, "Robert, you have an unusual quest for learning." All of his relatives were farmers and naturally he had assumed that he, too, would become a farmer. But that comment and her encouragement inspired Bobb to go to college and finish several degrees. To date, he has written eight books. Without her support, he probably would not have considered college. Her belief in him was pivotal in the direction of his entire life.

So, take time for others.

A phone call or card to assure friends of your prayers may be the encouragement they need to hear which may make the difference in keeping them from feeling depressed. "You did so well; I'm proud of you," whispered in the ear of a child after a Christmas performance may be just the words he needs to feel that sense of approval when he is unsure of how he did.

You can tell someone who is grieving "I care" by sitting with them and simply holding their hand. So often our presence and our love is all that's needed to bring comfort.

The Bible tells us we are to encourage one another. Whose cheerleader are you? Be there for someone. Reach down, grab a hand, and pull someone up. You can do that no matter what stage of life you are in or how much education or money you have or don't have. To fill someone else's cup will actually help to fill yours.

Think through the seven areas of life. You don't need to give equal weight to each area every season or year, but each area at least deserves to be considered. Again—be creative, don't let your season limit you unnecessarily.

Regardless of the stage in which you find yourself, if you are married, take the time to work on that relationship. Outside of your relationship with God, your marriage relationship is of highest importance. The Bible doesn't tell us to leave our parents and cling to our children, does it? But it does tell us to transfer our love and loyalties from our parents to our spouses.

I urge you to take the time to cultivate and protect that relationship. Plan fun times together. If your budget is restricted use your creativity. A friend once said to me, "If the grass is greener on the other side of the fence, try watering the grass on your own side of the fence." A fulfilling marriage requires hard work and effort but the results are well worth it.

While it's true that we can never control how another person responds to us or feels about us, we can put our focus on continuing to grow and develop spiritually, emotionally, and intellectually. We can take care of our physical appearance.

You were irresistible enough to attract your spouse—be fascinating enough to keep him. Perhaps he is a godly man and would never leave you because of the biblical prohibitions, but do what you can to assure that he never wishes he could. If your marriage is struggling today, ask your pastor or trusted friend for help.

A blank YEARLY FOCUS chart appears on pages 166 and 167. Again, this chart applies to the years you have remaining within this season. Fill it out using your completed SEASONS OF LIFE chart. Consider each priority carefully. Does it fit best in this particular year? Can you turn it into a measurable goal?

Some years you may not have any goals in some areas of your life—that's okay. Set goals you're comfortable with.

What Should I Do This Quarter?

Each year is divided into quarters and each quarter needs goals of its own. Determine which yearly goals you would like to tackle this quarter. The QUARTERLY FOCUS chart addresses the question: "If I am to accomplish my yearly goals, which of them should I plan to reach this particular quarter?" Study the sample QUARTERLY FOCUS chart on pages 104 and 105 before filling out the Quarterly Focus chart on pages 168 and 169.

Again, be realistic; don't over commit yourself. Be aware of seasonal holidays, vacations, guests who are planning to visit—all of which require time and may preclude other commitments. For instance, during the last quarter of the year most

QUARTERLY FOCUS

QUARTER>	*January–March*	*April–June*
SPIRITUAL	*Keep focused on God* *15 minutes daily personal time with God*	*Keep focused on God* *15 minutes daily personal time with God*
FAMILY/ MARRIAGE	*Prepare #1 child for #2's birth* *Weekend away with husband*	*Prepare #1 child for #2's birth* *Weekend away with husband*
PROFESSIONAL/ MENTAL		
PHYSICAL		
FINANCIAL	*Tithe to church* *Save for baby expenses*	*Tithe to church* *Save for baby expenses*
PERSONAL DEVELOPMENT		
SOCIAL/ FRIENDS	*Dinner and evening out with friends once a month*	*Dinner and evening out with friends once a month*

July–September	*October–December*	<QUARTER
Keep focused on God 15 minutes daily personal time with God	Keep focused on God 15 minutes daily personal time with God	**SPIRITUAL**
Give birth to child #2	Adjust to having 2 children	**FAMILY/ MARRIAGE**
		PROFESSIONAL/ MENTAL
	Begin exercise to get weight back to normal	**PHYSICAL**
Tithe to church Added baby expenses	Tithe to church Added baby expenses	**FINANCIAL**
		PERSONAL DEVELOPMENT
Dinner and evening out with friends once a month	Dinner and evening out with friends once a month	**SOCIAL/ FRIENDS**

women are busy preparing holiday dinners for Thanksgiving, Christmas, and New Year's Day. Holiday shopping and decorating consume everyone's time. It's probably not a good idea to plan to remodel your home during that quarter. But you may fulfill some of your social goals by hosting a holiday party. The last quarter is often the most hectic. Many women dread the holidays—but I believe this type of planning minimizes our stress and enhances our pleasure and sense of well-being.

What Should I Do This Week?

The WEEKLY FOCUS chart answers the question, "If I am to accomplish my quarterly goals, which of them should I focus on this particular week?" If you want to accomplish your quarterly goals, take each one and plug it into a week. You will need three of these, one for each month of the quarter. These charts can be completed one quarter at a time, just before the quarter begins. Each one should be reviewed the week before it begins. Study the sample WEEKLY FOCUS chart on pages 108 and 109. Then fill out the blank WEEKLY FOCUS on pages 170 and 171.

Each time you update a chart, ask yourself if your life, seasonal, and yearly goals are still what you desire them to be. Pray about them and be open to change. As God chisels you into the image of Christ, your desires and values may change.

Don't confuse this weekly chart with a weekly "to do" list. The chart articulates your *focus* for the week. For example, the week of Thanksgiving, my weekly focus simply says, "Thanksgiving Dinner."

The week preceding Christmas may say "Finish Christmas shopping." This is not the place for specifics.

What Shall I Do Today?

Daily goals should be established one week at a time, just before the week begins. Review each day's focus the day or night before. (Daily goals will be discussed more in the next chapter.)

Again, I'm not talking about the daily "to do" list, but rather a general focus for the day—an overall theme. It may be cleaning, laundry, or rest. If you are a career woman, perhaps it will list "studying reports from last month's general ledger" or "reviewing the Jones account." Having a daily focus eliminates the question "What shall I do today?" When the week's work seems like an insurmountable mountain, break it into workable days which melt those mountains into climbable molehills.

If you follow the guidelines in this chapter, you will be in control of your life rather than having it be in control of you.

WEEKLY FOCUS

WEEK>	*Dec. 29-Jan. 6*	*Jan. 7-13*
SPIRITUAL	*15 minutes daily personal time with God*	*15 minutes daily personal time with God*
FAMILY/ MARRIAGE	*Make trip plans for weekend away*	*Arrange babysitting for weekend away*
PROFESSIONAL/ MENTAL		
PHYSICAL		
FINANCIAL		*$50 savings for baby expenses*
PERSONAL DEVELOPMENT		
SOCIAL/ FRIENDS		

Jan. 14-20	*Jan. 21-27*	*Jan. 28-Feb.3*
15 minutes daily personal time with God	15 minutes daily personal time with God	15 minutes daily personal time with God
Weekend away with husband		Buy bigger bed for child #1
	$50 savings for baby expenses	Pay for new bed
Invite friends to dinner & evening out	Make arrangements for dinner reservations, babysitter	Dinner & evening out with friends

1. Whose cheerleader are you? Who is your cheerleader? Has one person stood out in your life as your personal encourager?

2. What are you doing at this point in your life to get "oxygen" for yourself so you can in turn meet other people's needs?

3. If you could only do one thing in your life, what would it be? How can you use your creativity to realize that dream? Brainstorm in the group to expand your thinking in this area.

4. Have goals ever represented failure to you? When did they represent success?

5. What are you feeling overwhelmed by that you could break down into workable units and experience progress as you complete steps along the way?

Section 3

Getting Through the Lists

7

Living with a Notebook

IF YOU BLINDFOLDED my father-in-law, twirled him around until he was dizzy, led him through a deep and unfamiliar woods and asked him when the sun was straight overhead which way was north, his arm would point as accurately north as that of a compass needle. He doesn't need a compass—I do. I need one to find my way when I'm in the woods and I need a "compass" to give direction to my daily life. That's why I have a notebook system.

It helps me:

✧ remember to call for my six month dental check-up without a reminder from the dentist;

✧ remember to send birthday cards to friends and family;

✧ remember when to fertilize my plants with what food;

✧ remember to take the car in for servicing;

✧ remember when my husband's flight arrives at which airport on which airline and what flight number;

✧ remember when we had our last tetanus shots;

✧ remember my husband's social security number and our credit card account numbers;

✧ and much more.

I need a notebook system.

Our lives are not simple. Our brains can easily overload. I can't speak for you, but I need help, and since you chose to read this book, I'm assuming you do, too. When putting together your notebook, answer the following questions.

What Level of Detail Do I Need?

Not everyone needs or can use the same notebook system. To a large extent your responsibilities in life at this particular time determine your needs. Generally speaking, the more details or activities you're responsible for, the more systemized, organized, and detailed your notebook needs to be.

If you're the mother of one toddler and have a housekeeper and a gardener, you may need only a place to keep a shopping list, names and addresses, and a small calendar. On the other hand, if you have five children ranging in age from five to seventeen and you are the PTA chairwoman, head of the annual bazaar at church, and teacher of a Sunday school class, you need a notebook with several tabs to keep track of the many details for which you are responsible.

When my children were small, my life focused around the needs of my family. I used a WEEKLY FOCUS chart and a monthly calendar to put in the few appointments I had. I kept the same WEEKLY

Focus chart at the beginning of my monthly calendar. It looked like this:

Monday:	Laundry and iron
Tuesday:	Clean upstairs
Wednesday:	Clean downstairs
Thursday:	Misc. appointments (i.e. Drs.) and catch up
Friday:	Plan meals and grocery shop
Saturday:	Family Day
Sunday:	Church and Family Day

This type of schedule helps to relieve the pressure that the duties of the week need to be done today. You may feel you "should" be doing grocery shopping when it is Monday—but you don't need to as that task will be done on Friday. On a Monday if you finish doing the laundry and ironing, relax and enjoy having accomplished what you set out to do. If the children are napping and you've already satisfied that day's focus, do something that gives you "oxygen" and don't feel guilty.

When your dentist calls for an appointment, make it on Thursday—that's the day of the week you've set aside for such things. Set aside blocks of time and don't expect yourself to do more than what belongs in that time period. There are always unforeseen things which may wipe out your plan for a day. Notice how I used Thursday to catch up. Be flexible.

Revise and adjust this schedule until it works for you. Once a successful routine is established, you don't need to spend time each morning figuring out what needs to be done.

My monthly calendar was sufficient for writing times for doctor appointments, etc. I did need tabs for various details to keep track of which we will discuss later, but the notebook was a small and simple one which fit into my pocketbook (or diaper bag) and was light to carry.

If your children are in school and you have become involved in several volunteer activities, you may need a daily calendar which lists the hours of the day down the left-hand column and lines where you can write in your appointments.

I used the Record Plate system for almost fifteen years. A strength of that system is found in the name and address setup. Because it is a multiring notebook, it allows for each person or family to have a separate small sheet of paper on which a tremendous amount of information can be kept. For instance, directions to their home, foods they especially like or dislike, birthdays of family members, dinners I served them so I wouldn't repeat the menu, correspondence, gifts exchanged, and so on.

The Day Runner System is probably the most accessible system available.[1] It is offered in all sizes and shapes and comes in a three-ring notebook. It can be adapted for your needs—simple or complex.

Choose your notebook carefully. Office supply or stationery stores offer a variety of notebook systems. Most of these have choices of tabs and pre-printed forms to accommodate your needs. Study them and choose one which best fits your situation.

Are You a Creator or a Maintainer?

Your personality type can also affect which type of notebook will best suit your needs. My husband developed an inventory which he calls the Role Preference Inventory. He explains that every project goes through several phases: the design phase, then the development of that design, and lastly the management of the project.

As each phase develops, different personalities enjoy that stage more than others. For instance, some people like to sit down with a blank piece of paper and create an idea for a project which they have never seen before. Other people don't have original ideas but like to take other people's ideas and develop them into a fully developed project. The people who design the project may be absolutely lost at knowing how to make it happen, whereas the people who thrive on developing it can stare at the wall for hours and never come up with an original design. Then, some people love to maintain the details of a project, refining it to a more effectively running system. Again, the people who maintain it have no idea how to develop it and less of an idea of how to originate it. The people who develop it are absolutely uninterested in or overwhelmed with the thought of maintaining it. Between and within each of the three project phases are places where people find their niche.

Do you know someone whose house is always a mess and who doesn't care if children are using crayons or finger paints to draw pictures wherever they choose around the house? The person is probably a designer and sees no real value in a spotless house but places tremendous worth on freedom of expression.

If you are one of those people, you may see little value in embracing the notebook in its totality. If you are a designer, I suspect you won't use this system because you will want to create your own. Use only those suggestions which suit you. I have no interest in making you feel guilty or telling you that you "should" complete each and every section. On the other hand, if you enjoy developing or maintaining a project, you will not only appreciate the value of a notebook, but the more detailed it is, the more you will embrace its features.

If you have been counting on your memory to keep track of your life and it isn't working, or if you write things down on little pieces of paper and find them weeks later in the pocket of a sweater, perhaps some sort of a notebook will help you. Use whatever helps you achieve the things you have decided are important.

It's critical to know and accept your own personality. Don't condemn yourself for who you are, and don't despise someone else for being different than you are. Be the person God has made you to be and give that freedom to your family and friends. First Peter 4:10-11 tells us that each of us is given different gifts to be used within the body of Christ:

> Each one should use whatever gift he has received to serve others, faithfully administering God's grace in its various forms. If anyone speaks, he should do it as one speaking the very words of God. If anyone

serves, he should do it with the strength God provides, so that in all things God may be praised through Jesus Christ. To him be the glory and the power for ever and ever.

The following system works for me. It's my compass, my road map, my "brain." If I use it, my dreams become realities. I'm able to say yes to what I have carefully chosen as my priorities and goals, and no to things of lesser priority.

My notebook is divided into three sections: FOCUS AND CALENDAR, PEOPLE AND PROJECTS, and DETAILS I NEED TO TRACK.

Focus and Calendar

Several years ago, when Bobb worked at World Vision International, we were close friends of his colleague and wife, Bill and Jean Needham. Bill's responsibilities included presenting to the president a daily summary of world events which might be of interest to World Vision. Bill did outstanding work, he never seemed to be in a hurry, never appeared overwhelmed, and always seemed to have his pulse rate set on "normal." When Bobb inquired as to his secret, Bill gave the following analogy.

He said he considered his schedule like an egg basket and the activities or responsibilities as the eggs. Since an egg basket will only hold a given number of eggs, there comes a point at which a new egg introduced to the basket will either fall, crashing to the floor itself, or cause another one to be the Humpty Dumpty.

Bill explained that when the president asked him to take on another responsibility, he would respond by saying he would be happy to do that for him, but presently his time schedule (egg basket) was full, and proceed to ask which of his other responsibilities (eggs) would he want him to postpone, delegate, or ignore in order to complete this new one.

I will take the analogy one step further. At various seasons in our lives, our egg baskets are different sizes, or are shaped distinctively, accommodating differing numbers or sizes of eggs. At times, one or two eggs can be heavy and even though the basket looks rather empty to other people, adding even one more small egg would make it impossible for the owner to carry.

Only you can determine which eggs and how many eggs are appropriate and comfortable for your basket.

What Goes in This Section? How Do I Use It?

You may be wondering where to put all the charts you've been filling out. If your notebook is very small, you may not have room to keep them in it. I suggest keeping them in a file that is accessible. If your charts contain confidential information, be sure that you keep the file in a secure place.

Your LIFE FOCUS chart and SEASON OF LIFE charts don't have to be in your notebook. However, I recommend that you keep your yearly, quarterly, and weekly goals in your notebook for easy reference.

Here are some ways to maximize your use of this section as you focus on the week ahead:

Try to organize the days of your week before it begins. Get as many details in on Saturday or Sunday night as you can. You already established the focus for the week and for each day. Now is the time to finalize those particulars. What do you want to do each day?

Start with the non-negotiable. These may be athletic games of your children, parent-teacher conferences, and other events or appointments at which you need to appear but have no control over the appointed time.

Plug in the things you must do over which you control the time or day. Dental appointments and grocery shopping are examples. You may decide to designate one day per week for such appointments or errands to keep every day from seeming to be chopped up into bits and pieces.

After you have scheduled the non-negotiable items, pull out your WEEKLY FOCUS to see what else you may have time to do today. What did you put on your WEEKLY FOCUS chart that fits the time block that is available to you today? If this is your day for errands, you may not have any time available. Move on to the next day and evaluate the time available.

Remember...

1. Guard your calendar carefully. It represents where you will spend your precious and limited time. Because you are given a restricted amount of time on this earth, it is up to you to determine where and how you will spend it. If you allow other people to impose their priorities on your time, you will eventually resent those people and feel robbed because your own goals are not met.

On the other hand, do leave time for unexpected interruptions so that when someone really needs you, you are able to be available.

You already asked God to make clear to you what is the best use of your time by establishing significant goals. Now do what you need to do to make time for the realization of those priorities and goals.

Some of you reading this book will find this organization to be freeing, relieving your fears of forgetting something important or not getting everything done. Others will find it confining and inhibiting to your spontaneity. I would suggest that you read and carefully consider all of the options. Then choose what best meets your needs.

You are human and not a machine. *You can't do everything.* Only do what is "best" and of greatest importance to you.

2. You don't have time to waste. Learn the distinction between rest, play, and waste. God commands us to get rest for our bodies. We actually accomplish more if we take that time to rest and relax than if we work our bodies continuously without resting them. *It is not a waste of time for you to take a nap if you are tired.*

Within each of us lives a child, no matter what our age. I love a roller coaster, a slide, a swing, and Disneyland. I stand (I should say swim!) in awe of God's creation as I scuba dive. Next year I want to parachute from a plane. I've been told the exhilaration of the free fall is beyond description. This type of diversion from the intensity we experience as we stretch toward reaching our goals is play, and it's necessary.

However, none of us has time to waste. According to Webster, waste is "to use up or spend without real need, gain, or purpose; squander; to wear away; consume gradually; use up." Rest has a purpose. Play has a purpose. To waste has no purpose or value.

What is considered play or rest for one person is wasteful for another. For example, when my head hits the pillow, an internal switch clicks off. I can drink fifteen cups of coffee and fall directly asleep when I lie down. My husband, however, seems to carry his thoughts to bed and the proverbial wheels of his brain continue to turn. The most effective way for him to coerce those wheels to a halt is to watch a detective show on television.

For him to watch that show under those circumstances is actually a necessity to get the rest he needs. For me to watch it by myself is a waste because I neither enjoy it nor does it serve any purpose or meet any need. But for me to watch it with him is a chance to hold his hand and share a bowl of popcorn with him. That changes it from a waste to a priority.

3. Don't let the "good" rob you of the "best." We all have lived under the tyranny of the urgent. It's especially difficult to select the best over the good when it comes to our daily calendars. When you establish your seasonal goals, you will not allow a "good" to waste a year of your life, but when you view a day, you rationalize that it's only one day. What does that matter in a lifetime? That is valid reasoning if it is just one day, but it is too easy for that to happen consistently, and before we realize it, a week has passed. We look back in disappointment because we have accomplished nothing of significant value.

If this happens, try to re-establish the procedures and goals. One day or a week off the schedule doesn't mean failure.

Having your calendar already scheduled with what is "best" for you allows you to say no more easily to a request for a "good." If you vaguely plan sometime this week to do a "best," when a request for a "good" comes along, you may be coerced into accepting it because of an open spot in your calendar. That may keep you from accomplishing your "best."

An example of this might be your desire to visit your neighbor who is in the hospital. You believe that to be a "best," but have not, as yet, scheduled it on your calendar. Let's suppose another friend calls and asks you to ride with her to pick up her mail order which has just arrived at the store, some distance away. Since nothing is on your calendar at the moment, you agree to go and don't return for two hours. As you study your week that evening, you see that was the only time during the week you could have visited your neighbor. The "good" robbed you of the "best."

On the other side of the coin, perhaps the friend who called wanting you to ride with her is having marital problems and needs your listening ear and counsel. Riding with her may be the very best use of your time for that day. Conceivably a phone call to your hospitalized friend will be sufficient. When an opportunity arises, evaluate its importance for your day and be willing to be flexible to move your schedule to accommodate unforeseen opportunities which may even be better than what you originally perceived to be the best for that day.

Projects and People

The tab sections in this part of your notebook will vary with individual situations. Here are some tabs that I have used. Use these or create the tabs which are most helpful for you.

1. *Family and Marriage* can contain lists of entertainment ideas, places to visit, or amusement parks you all enjoy. It might include an ongoing list of gifts which family members mention they would enjoy. Write them down so you won't forget them when Christmas or a birthday approaches.

2. _____'s *Classroom* might be a valuable tab if you are a room mother. It could include a list of all students in the class with their mother or father's first names and phone numbers. It might include dates of class field trips and lists of the mothers that will accompany you or make a desert.

3. I usually include a *Notes and Ideas* tab for a place to write down an idea or take notes on an interesting speaker. It could also be called *Sermon Notes* or *Bible Study Class Notes*.

4. My husband gets a section of his own. He travels extensively, but he calls home each evening. In this section I write down anything of

either personal or business nature about which we need to speak. When we discuss it, I write down the appropriate action necessary and when completed, check it off the list.

I also include issues we need to discuss at length or decisions to be made. As we drive in the car or fly together and have blocks of unscheduled time, I open my notebook to this section to jog my memory of topics to address.

5. I have found it to be very helpful to have a *Menus* section. If you will use this time-saving method, you can eliminate hours spent writing out menus and grocery lists. The next time you choose a menu, write it down as usual but on a piece of paper which fits into your notebook. Then on the back, put the list of ingredients required to make this menu. Each time you prepare a different menu, repeat the same procedure. Choose your menu carefully around your main dish for color, food texture, compatibility of tastes, etc. Soon you will have many carefully formulated menus from which to choose. When you have completed it once, you never need to repeat it again. Each time you serve the main dish, you repeat the same side dishes with it. Your grocery list has already been made.

You can call me organized or lazy, whichever the case may be, but I dislike repeating the same activity when it isn't necessary. Be creative with other things you do to save precious time. And have a great time with the time you save.

6. I have recently added a tab which is a temporary one for this year entitled *Move*. Included in

it are lists of phone numbers of real estate agents, utility companies, phone companies, etc.

Create your own tab sections to custom fit your needs—you may need more or you may need less. This notebook is to help you.

Details I Need to Track

Most of us need a place to keep track of details. However, what we need to keep track of varies with individuals, so again, customize it to fit your own needs. Below are listed some details found in my personal notebook.

1. Personal and Medical Information. Having this information at my fingertips saves me literally hundreds of hours of unnecessarily searching for information.

Each member of my family has a separate sheet of paper. On it I include information such as:

Birth date;
Driver's license;
Social Security number;
Blood type;
Life insurance policies;
Medical insurance policy;
Auto insurance company and numbers;
Clothing sizes;
Passport number;
Allergies;
Immunization record;
Checking account number;
Safe deposit box number;
Airline frequent flyer numbers.

Keeping a record of the immunizations of your children saves you trips or phone calls to the doctor when the children begin or change schools or in case of an accident. If any special medical problems occur in your family, a list of doctors with phone numbers, and a record of activity is absolutely invaluable.

2. Financial. If you adhere to a budget, your expenditures are logged here. A simple current ledger sheet saves you considerable time as you total numbers at the end of the month or quarter when the facts are cold.

Keeping track of tax deductible items in this section is beneficial. Recording expenditures such as medical payments, contributions, interest payments, and miscellaneous deductible taxes as incurred will save you many hours at the end of the year. Simply totaling columns in this itemized ledger keeps you from reviewing each separate checkbook register searching for allowable deductions at the end of the year or at tax time.

3. Shopping. If you don't need a grocery list, you are truly amazing! Keep a current list updated as you run out of items, and then add to that list as you plan menus.

You may also wish to keep a separate list of other miscellaneous items which you need to purchase other than at the grocery store. This would include birthday cards, or a gift item which needs to be purchased. Keeping a list prevents frustration and the lingering thought that something of importance is forgotten.

4. Phone Lists. A list of phone numbers can be as detailed as you wish. You may wish to keep separate lists for family, business, and friends. Another way is to keep lists by groups of people. Baby-sitters, people who serve on a committee with you, other mothers in your child's classroom, your supervisor, and fellow employees are a few. It's an easy reference to look up the group where all the numbers are listed and eliminates the need to find numbers which are listed individually by alphabet.

5. "To Do" List. Keep a list of things which have no specific deadline but need to be done whenever it is possible or convenient. They are things you don't want to forget, and you'll get to as soon as you can. If you have an extra hour, look at the list, see if you can start anything, work on it, or finish within that time frame.

This list is never completed because you are always adding to it. Let it be a help in remembering these important items. Don't feel a lack of completion that the list is never finished; it's not intended to be.

6. Special Dates to Remember. Every year there are specific dates we need to remember: birthdays, anniversaries of special friends, special memories to celebrate. On page 133, you will find a sample of such a page to record these special times. This page is also effective for keeping track of seasonal dates to remember such as yard and garden maintenance, months to fertilize certain plants or spray for insects, months to change the furnace filter or months to turn over the mattress. Anything you need to remember to do at the same time each year can be recorded on this page.

Keep Control

I had a college professor who advised, "Don't let a budget control you; you control your budget. Make it work for you."

I have the same advice for your notebook. Don't let it control you; you control it. Don't let it be just one more thing of which you need to keep track. Let it help you keep control of your life. If it isn't working for you, change it until it does. Make it fully yours to meet your individual needs.

Be prepared to adjust your notebook as you use it. Chances are you have rearranged your kitchen cupboards more than once since you moved into your current home or apartment. As you worked in it you realized that another configuration would save you steps or be more convenient. Just so, as you work with your notebook, make changes which make your life easier.

There are many personal notebook and time management systems available at office supply, stationery, or specialty stores. If your system doesn't have everything you need, draw from different systems. If needed, hole punch theirs to fit yours or make up your own. Design a system which maximizes your abilities and efforts in reaching your carefully chosen goals.

Note

1. The Day Runner phone number is: 1-800-635-5544. They will send you an exhaustive catalog.

SPECIAL DATES TO REMEMBER

DAY-FOCUS™

JANUARY

FEBRUARY

MARCH

APRIL

MAY

JUNE

Day-Focus™ Form: 4-0-08-689

1. Are you currently using a notebook system? Are you happy with it? What do you like best about it?

2. What details do you need to keep track of which you can visualize benefiting you by fitting into your notebook? If you tend to write things on scraps of paper and lose them, what categories or tabs best fit your needs to organize those details?

3. What are some special dates to remember each year that you can benefit by recording here?

4. What is lacking in your notebook system which would help maximize your efforts in reaching your goals? How can you be creative in obtaining this tool?

8

Time- and Stress-Saving Tips

THE PRINCIPLE of this book—define a task and break it down into workable units—is applicable to many areas of life. I encourage you to examine different tasks which you may not enjoy and see if applying these principles brings relief.

One of the annual unpleasant and dreaded responsibilities I have is preparing our taxes. I love to work with people, and it is sheer discipline for me to sit behind a desk and fill out forms. I despise figuring taxes. Taxes, to me, are a Mt. Everest I have to climb annually.

A few years ago I had a particularly busy year and it was the middle to the end of March before I even looked at the general ledger to begin the compilation of numbers for Uncle Sam. When I could procrastinate no longer, I spread the necessary documents out on my desk, and surveyed the forms which were to be completed—fifteen in all.

As I stared at the blank forms before me, it dawned on me—the individual forms were the workable units into which the mountain of taxes could be broken. If I completed one form each day, I could finish the task in fifteen days. No sweat. One form a day was easy. I was almost looking forward to doing it. I knew I would get it done. I took the long dark tunnel with no end in sight and transformed it into fifteen short tunnels—each with a glimmer of light at the end.

Each day, after I completed a form, I felt a sense of accomplishment. I had fulfilled my plan for that day, and didn't feel the burden of not having completed the entire project. In two weeks the job was completed.

Those Giant Projects

I began chapter 6 by telling you how stressed I was about our move until I planned it. I put into practice the principle of taking a large project and breaking it down into workable units.

I actually started by making two "to do" lists: one for California, the other for Florida. Then beside each item I listed which month I wanted to complete this particular detail.

Next, I sorted the list by month so that everything I needed to do in May, for example, was grouped under that month. Then I divided the months into weeks and listed what I wanted to accomplish that week. For example what was May was now May 2 or May 9 depending on which week I wanted to work on it. Then I wrote it on my Weekly Focus chart.

Next, taking into consideration all the other things which were already on my agenda, I wrote in names and dates for taking friends out for a good-bye lunch. Because I scheduled these things far in advance, I had time to work everything into my agenda. If I had waited until the month before the move, it would have been impossible for me to have packed, had the utilities turned off, arranged for the moving van, had five teas for friends, taken seven friends to lunch, eight couples to dinner, and accomplished all the other details which were on my list.

Notice, I did make some choices. I couldn't invite every friend over. I chose to do what was best. I've included my list on pages 148 through 150 to show you how this type of planning is done.

If you have a large project looming over you:

1. Make an exhaustive "to do" list.
2. Beside each item, write the month in which you want to get it done.
3. Prioritize it by the week within that month to do it.
4. Write it on your daily calendar a week ahead of schedule.

Apply these steps and you can do anything... well, almost.

That Toughest Quarter

The busiest time of year is the fall when the holidays approach. Many women dread this time of year because of the added stress. But with proper planning, I think it's possible to enjoy this festive time.

Let's do a quarterly plan together. Put on your Christmas music and let's get started.

Someone quoted an "expert" who claimed that women spend more time planning Christmas than they do the rest of their lives. Perhaps that is true of you, or perhaps Christmas is one of those seasons in which you find yourself harried and frazzled, never seeming to get everything finished. By planning Christmas ahead, you will have time to focus on Jesus, the real meaning of Christmas. It will become more enjoyable as you take control of the details of the season. You don't have to be a "wonder woman" to accomplish everything that you most want to do or that is your best choice.

For the sake of example to demonstrate how this system can work practically in your life, I'd like to propose a generic Christmas countdown. Please revise it for your use if it is helpful to you. Get out your calendar and start working your details into my suggestions.

Let's begin with a partial list of our quarterly goals: October through December.

- Serve Thanksgiving dinner.
- Attend husband's office party.
- Shop for Christmas gifts.
- Purchase and send Christmas cards.
- Decorate house.
- Serve Christmas dinner to extended family.

Now let's move to the week of Thanksgiving Dinner and look at our weekly goals:

November 20:   *Thanksgiving dinner.*
                Decorate for Christmas.

November 27:   *Make Christmas lists.*
                Buy Christmas cards.

December 4:   *Send Christmas cards.*
               Begin gift shopping.

December 11:   *Finish gift shopping.*
               Organize Christmas dinner.

December 18:   *Shop for Christmas Dinner.*
               Attend office party.

December 25:   *Merry Christmas.*
               Serve Christmas Dinner.

Now for the daily schedule. Of course, I am only putting in the Christmas plans and not taking into account the other responsibilities that you have. The final time balances are critical at this point. Don't over schedule yourself in any one day. Try to distribute things equally so that no single day carries a disproportionate amount of the load. Let's pick up the schedule the day after Thanksgiving:

November 24:   *Decorate the house for Christmas.*
               Buy Poinsettias.

November 25:   *Plant Poinsettias and finish*
               decorating.

November 26:   *REST.*

November 27:   *Compile children's lists.*

November 28:   *Compile husband's and my lists.*

November 29:   *Collect lists from relatives.*

November 30:   *Purchase Christmas cards and*
               stamps.

November 31:   *Mark address lists for cards sent.*

December 1: *Make lists of friends to be given gifts and lists of gifts. Make lists of shopping areas and which gifts to purchase where.*

December 2: *Start addressing cards.*

December 3: *REST.*

December 4: *Address more cards.*

December 5: *Finish addressing cards—send.*

December 6: *Order gifts from catalogues.*

December 7: *Shop at wholesale membership club.*

December 8: *Shop at local mall.*

December 9: *Shop at swap meet.*

December 10: *REST.*

December 11: *Finish gift shopping—specialty shops, misc.*

December 12: *Wrap presents and put under tree.*

December 13: *Organize Christmas dinner menu.*

December 14: *Make grocery list for Christmas dinner.*

December 15: *Catch up on anything that didn't get done.*

December 16: *Take the kids Christmas shopping.*

December 17: *REST.*

December 18: *Catch up on details missed, meet friends for lunch.*

December 19: *Relax. Do non-Christmas projects.*

December 20: *Free time.*

December 21: *Shop for Christmas dinner.*

December 22: *Attend Christmas party.*

December 23: *Get stockings ready.*

December 24: *REST.*

December 25: *Merry Christmas. Gifts are opened. Dinner is served.*

If you allow the shopping and other activities to be delayed until the last minute, you will feel considerable pressure. By using this planning system to break the tasks down into workable units, no day becomes overwhelming. In fact, several days are planned with nothing to do that involves Christmas. You could also make Christmas gifts throughout the year. If so your first quarter might include something such as making an afghan for Susie.

Time-Saving Tips

This book wouldn't be complete without a few general tips on saving time: The principle is simple—combine things that require thinking with things that don't, or things that require your presence (flying in an airplane) with things that require your attention (cross stitching or letter writing). Make a list of things you might be able to do during otherwise unoccupied time.

1. *Learn to accomplish more than one thing at a time.* For example, keep a book, which you have chosen as one you would like to read, in your car. As you sit in the doctor's waiting room with a sick child, don't find yourself at the mercy of the receptionist who has subscribed to magazines she chose.

Get your book from your car and read what you choose to read. If the child isn't too sick, use this time to talk to him or her to catch up on necessary news or to explore new ideas. Use the time to listen and discuss.

Another time when you can do two things at once is when you're talking on the phone. There are "brainless" routine tasks that if planned for can be realized during this time. For instance, I use this time to decorate plain paper, which is scrap ends of business printing, with a favorite rose or boarder stamp. It is nothing which requires my thinking, and so I am not distracted from the conversation.

A friend keeps magazines near the phone and browses them, dog-earring pages of articles she would like to read when she is waiting at the doctor's office, or in the car for her son to finish up his soccer practice.

Another friend has a business of making and painting wooden necklaces. When she budgets time to paint, she also catches up on her phone calls and keeps contact with friends.

Many people now have portable phones. This allows them to make beds, do laundry, clean up the kitchen, etc. while talking on the phone.

2. *Keep tapes in your car which you may have listed in the "Personal Growth" column.* As you drive down the freeway alone, listen to them rather than a radio program which may be of no value or interest to you.

3. *When you cook, double the recipe and freeze the part you don't use for a later time.* I've spent three

days in preparation of dinners which were to be served over the next three weeks. The first day was spent deciding on the menus, the second in compiling a combined grocery list and purchasing the ingredients, and the third day I spent in the kitchen preparing the meals.

As the sauce for the lasagna simmered for five hours I cooked rice and sautéed the scallions for stuffed cabbage leaves. While the scallions were sautéing, I grated cheese for the next entree. By the end of the day, my freezer was full. When guests and relatives stayed for a prolonged visit, I put the dinner in the pre-set oven before we left in the morning, so that as we walked in the door that evening, the dinner entree was ready.

4. *Set up a simple filing system which will give you a great return for your time invested.* When I have a few extra moments as I'm browsing in the stationery store I sometimes see cards I like but don't need right then. However, I purchase them and place them in my file for cards. The file is divided into groupings of cards for "Friendship," "Birthday," "Get Well," "Anniversary," and so on.

It took me thirty minutes to set up that system. When I return home from purchasing cards, it takes me no more than three minutes to file the new cards I have acquired. When I hear of a friend's illness, it takes me all of about thirty seconds to find a suitable card to send.

Without such a system it may take me thirty minutes to sort through a box of cards to find the ideal choice—and much longer if had to go to the store for each occasion. That short time I spent setting up that system has saved me many hours of time and frustration through the years as well as kept me in close contact with my friends.

5. *Use a "tickler system" that not only is a time-saving help but assurance of keeping you from forgetting to pay bills or sending important documents on time.* Keep a plastic see-through folder by the phone or a daily frequented spot in your home with envelopes sorted by due date to send, the next to be mailed being in front. When a bill comes in the mail, put the date to be sent where the stamp will go and file it in the plastic envelope. Since you see the file daily you will not likely overlook mailing those important envelopes.

6. *Develop a time-saving travel system.* When I read a magazine article about an interesting place I'd like to visit, I tear out the article and file it in the folder which bears the name of that city or country. When I am planning our next trip, I don't have to spend time searching for the article. Interesting information on the particular country or city we wish to visit is in one handy folder at my fingertips.

7. *Arrange your calendar a month in advance.* As a friend plans her calendar a month in advance, she calls her favorite baby-sitter and arranges for her to sit on those particular nights when she will be out. Since very few women are so organized, she has top priority with her choice of sitters. It also saves her time to make one call for the month rather than one call per evening out.

8. *Learn to save lists that you make which can be used repeatedly.* List articles to pack for camping

trips, places to go when out-of-town guests visit, information for baby-sitters, and directions to infrequently visited places. If you have a computer, you may want to store this information there rather than carrying it with you in your notebook.

You now have the focus you need and the tools you need to manage your life. Remember, if you get lost in the forest, don't continue to run blindly in circles. Look at your North Star. Focus. Get direction. You'll find your way out of the forest—and enjoy the beauty along the way.

MOVING TO DO LIST

April

Make list of friends to say good-bye to and
    how 4/18
Put to do on quarterly calendar 4/18
Make to do list 4/18
Prioritize to do list 4/18
Put to do on weekly calendar 4/25
Put to do on daily calendar 4/12

May

Take friend to good-bye lunch—Jerri 5/1
Pack—CA 5/17
Couple to good-bye dinner—Trotter 5/28

June

Friend to good-bye lunch—Dawn 6/14
Pack—CA 6/14
Couple to good-bye dinner—Berg 6/19

July

Couple to good-bye dinner—7/
Friend to good-bye lunch—7/
Pack—CA 7/
Good-bye tea 7/

August

Couple to good-bye dinner—8/
Friend to good-bye lunch—8/
Pack—CA 8/
Good-bye tea 8/

September

Find a house and purchase—FL 9/
Couple to good-bye dinner—9/
Arrange financing for house—FL 9/
Pack—CA 9/
Friend to good-bye lunch—9/
Good-bye tea 9/

October

Good-bye tea 10/
Friend to good-bye lunch—10/
Couple to good-bye dinner—10/
Pack—CA 10/

November

Good-bye tea 11/
Set up checking account—FL 11/
Pack—CA 11/
Couple to good-bye dinner—11/
Address change notices 11/
Transfer auto insurance prem. to FL bank 11/
Friend to good-bye lunch 11/
Friend to good-bye lunch 11/

December

Join church—FL 12/
Drivers' licenses—FL 12/
Get doctors arranged in FL 12/
Homeowner's insurance—FL 12/
CA Phone# fwd to FL phone# 12/
Friend to good-bye lunch—12/
Pack—CA 12/
Cancel rental property contents—CA 12/
Change address passport—CA 12/
Have medical files sent to new doctors—CA 12/
Garage sale—CA 12/
Get new phone #—FL 12/
Arrange moving van—CA 12/

January

Connect utilities—FL 1/
Set up voter registration—FL 1/
Estate sales for furniture—? 1/
Car registration—FL 1/
Unpack—FL 1/

Invite to Tea Before I Move

Former Church Friends

Linda Elliott A
Jeni Taylor A
Patsy Bogan A
Carley Georgioff A
Judi Baugh A

Women's Ministry Council

Bonnie Masters B
Christen Abbott B
Beth Mount B
Robin Chadwick B
Noelle Olkowski B

Other Church Friends

Jan Hallof C
Rachael Bradley C
Camille Osterkamp C
Connie Grimaud C
Tricia Raz C

Growth Group Ladies

Kathie Rogers D
Johnna Harsany D
Liz Halliday D
Allison Foust D

Other Friends

Crystal Knudeson E
Eileen Blom E
Shawna Anderson E
Tana Derocher E
Lylah Harris E
DeLoy Bohrer E

Invite to Lunch Before I Move

Virginia Brant—6/14
Chris Quinones
Rachel Parrish
Karen McMichael
Dawn Roberts—4/30
Diane Collins
Jerri Traphagen

Couples to Invite to Dinner Before We Move

Micah and Irene Morgan
Ryan and Jan Lloyd and kids
Paul and Joyce Goodmanson
Marty and Cindy Hoffner
Charlie and Vanessa Berg
George and Alice Henry
Benjamin and Laura Gillespie
Mark and Robin Trotter—5/28

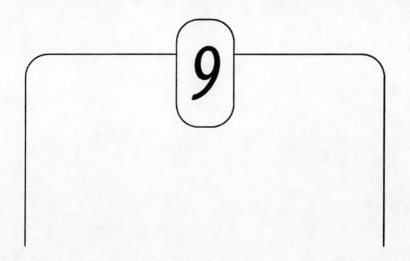

9

Plenty of Time

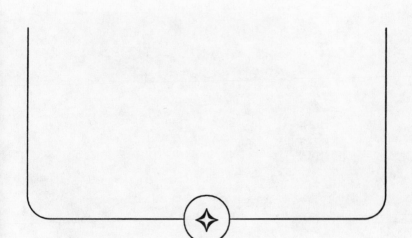

IT'S TRUE—you can't do everything. But you can do what is best for *you*.

It may take you many hours or days to consider carefully the choices available to you, and to make wise decisions concerning your commitments. But the time you spend creating a future plan pales by comparison to the time you could waste without such a design. Take the time necessary to ensure that your choices are the best. I hope this book is helping you sort out what you *can* do—what is *best* and most important for you.

Even after you've established a strategy, it's easy to get out of balance. Give yourself enough room and flexibility to accommodate unforeseeable circumstances. If your child gets sick or a temporary volunteer position takes an unexpected amount of time, you'll find your "to do" list backed up. To keep on target in reaching your goals, simply refocus as quickly as possible.

When we returned home from Europe with my parents, I didn't need to revise my lifetime vision, for it hadn't changed. I didn't revise my annual priorities; those hadn't changed. But I *did* rework and revise my quarterly priorities and then my weekly and daily goals. Within a few hours, I had refocused; I was back on target. It was a revised plan, and it worked. I completed this book and all my other "to do's" from my list of forty-three items.

You can do the same.

Make annual, quarterly, and weekly adjustments. Even if nothing unforeseen gets you off track, your priorities may change as new challenges come your way or situations change. Be flexible. Maintain your daily focus as you meet with God. Work hard, play passionately, and rest completely.

My pastor once commented, "At the end of my life, I don't want to look back and wonder what my life would have looked like if I had done it God's way." I trust this book has influenced your thinking so that at the end of your life you will smile with satisfaction, knowing you made good choices. You did what you believed pleased God.

Follow the plan in this book:

1. Establish your lifelong priorities.
2. Confirm your season of life.
3. Set priorities for your yearly goals for that season.
4. Decide which quarter you will work on each of those yearly goals.
5. Set weekly goals that accommodate the quarterly goals.
6. Create or organize a daily agenda.

After you complete this list, you will experience daily gratification, knowing that you are on target for accomplishing what you want to do over your entire lifetime.

Sometimes it's difficult to differentiate our motives in relationship to our goals. As Christian women, your desires must be to please God, yet we have personal preferences as human beings. Are these mutually exclusive? Is it acceptable to choose what I, as a human woman, prefer doing?

The key is focus. Where is yours? Is it on pleasing God or yourself? Saturate yourself with God and allow Him to cultivate your individual creativity and to give you the desires of your heart.

If your focus is on God and you ask Him to help you to set your priorities and goals, He doesn't care what details you choose or how you accomplish them. He lets you fill in the details and the methods to accomplish the goals yourself. "In his heart a man plans his course, but the LORD determines his steps" (Proverbs 16:9).

I don't believe God cares what style of furniture you have as long as you don't become preoccupied with it rather than with Him. I don't believe you need to ask His permission to turn off the light switch or which grocery store to patronize. I believe He cares more about who you *are*—how you love Him and how you extend His love to the world—than what details you carefully plan in executing that focus.

If your focus is on Him, you can relax and rely on Him to change your direction if He has something specifically in mind for you to do other than what you're currently planning. Solomon tells us in Proverbs to make plans counting on God to direct us.

Have you gone to the tower even as Habakkuk went to search for God's perspective? I trust you journeyed there and sought God's wisdom for a plan for your life. That is the first and most critical step in securing a significant future.

By using the principles of this book you can say yes to that "best" plan and no to other "good" things which would distract you from that blueprint. I trust you will have courage to say no to things which would keep you from experiencing the life Jesus talked about when He said, "I have come that [you] may have life, and have it to the full" (John 10:10).

My prayer for you is that you live life to the full, that you experience God's incredible love for you, that you will smile with pleasure knowing that the choices you make please God—and please you, too.

I'd like to end with a prayer taken from an old book of pilgrim's prayers.

Lord, I have time;
I have plenty of time,
all the time you give me,
the years of my life,
the days of my years,
the hours of my days,
they are all mine.
Mine to fill, quietly, calmly,
but to fill completely, up to the brim,

to offer them back to you...
I am not asking you, Lord,
for time to do this and then that,
but for your grace to do conscientiously,
in the time that you give me,
what you enable me to do...
what *you* want me to do.

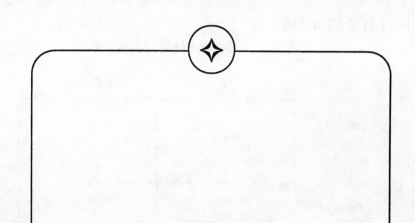

Appendix

LIFE FOCUS

Before I die, I want to...

	BE:	DO:
SPIRITUAL		
FAMILY/ MARRIAGE		
PROFESSIONAL/ MENTAL		
PHYSICAL		
FINANCIAL		
PERSONAL DEVELOPMENT		
SOCIAL/ FRIENDS		

LIFE FOCUS

Before I die, I want to...

HAVE:	HELP:	
		SPIRITUAL
		FAMILY/ MARRIAGE
		PROFESSIONAL/ MENTAL
		PHYSICAL
		FINANCIAL
		PERSONAL DEVELOPMENT
		SOCIAL/ FRIENDS

SEASONS OF LIFE

SEASON> OF LIFE	
SPIRITUAL	
FAMILY/ MARRIAGE	
PROFESSIONAL/ MENTAL	
PHYSICAL	
FINANCIAL	
PERSONAL DEVELOPMENT	
SOCIAL/ FRIENDS	

SEASONS OF LIFE

		<SEASON OF LIFE
		SPIRITUAL
		FAMILY/ MARRIAGE
		PROFESSIONAL/ MENTAL
		PHYSICAL
		FINANCIAL
		PERSONAL DEVELOPMENT
		SOCIAL/ FRIENDS

YEARLY FOCUS

YEAR>		
SPIRITUAL		
FAMILY/ MARRIAGE		
PROFESSIONAL/ MENTAL		
PHYSICAL		
FINANCIAL		
PERSONAL DEVELOPMENT		
SOCIAL/ FRIENDS		

166

SEASON:

		<YEAR
		SPIRITUAL
		FAMILY/ MARRIAGE
		PROFESSIONAL/ MENTAL
		PHYSICAL
		FINANCIAL
		PERSONAL DEVELOPMENT
		SOCIAL/ FRIENDS

167

QUARTERLY FOCUS

QUARTER>		
SPIRITUAL		
FAMILY/ MARRIAGE		
PROFESSIONAL/ MENTAL		
PHYSICAL		
FINANCIAL		
PERSONAL DEVELOPMENT		
SOCIAL/ FRIENDS		

168

YEAR:

		<QUARTER
		SPIRITUAL
		FAMILY/ MARRIAGE
		PROFESSIONAL/ MENTAL
		PHYSICAL
		FINANCIAL
		PERSONAL DEVELOPMENT
		SOCIAL/ FRIENDS

WEEKLY FOCUS

WEEK>	
SPIRITUAL	
FAMILY/ MARRIAGE	
PROFESSIONAL/ MENTAL	
PHYSICAL	
FINANCIAL	
PERSONAL DEVELOPMENT	
SOCIAL/ FRIENDS	

MONTH:

<table>
<tr><td></td><td></td><td></td></tr>
<tr><td></td><td></td><td></td></tr>
<tr><td></td><td></td><td></td></tr>
<tr><td></td><td></td><td></td></tr>
<tr><td></td><td></td><td></td></tr>
<tr><td></td><td></td><td></td></tr>
<tr><td></td><td></td><td></td></tr>
<tr><td></td><td></td><td></td></tr>
</table>

Suggested Books and Daily Studies

Bennett, Arthur. Editor. *The Valley of Vision.*
Edinburgh: The Banner of Truth Trust, 1975.

Chambers, Oswald. *My Utmost for His Highest.* New
York: Dodd, Mead & Company, 1935.

de Caussade, Jean-Pierre. *Abandonment to Divine
Providence.* Image Books. New York: Doubleday,
1975.

Ferguson, Sinclair. *A Heart for God.* Edinburgh:
Banner of Truth, 1987.

Hand, Thomas A. *Augustine on Prayer.* New York:
Catholic Book Publishing Co., 1963

Packer, J. I. *God's Words.* Grand Rapids, Mich.:
Baker Book House, 1981.

Packer, J. I. *Knowing God.* Illinois: InterVarsity Press,
1973.

Sproul, R. C. *Essential Truths of the Christian Faith.*
Wheaton, Ill.: Tyndale House Publishers, 1992.

Sproul, R. C. Jr. Editor. *Tabletalk.* Orlando, Fla.:
Ligonier Ministries, monthly publication.